Three Holy Kings

By

Gaby Kool

Note to the Reader: Three Holy Kings

To my children, grandchildren and great-grandchildren: Carmen, Jo-Ann, Joey, Nathalie, Gabriella, Isabella, Caesar, Christian, Emma, Preston, Sunny, Brooklyn, Landon, Ralphael and Angelia.

During Christmas of 2023 whilst we were celebrating Epiphany, it struck me that these three Kings were Middle Eastern and Asian Kings. The results of my research were indeed, Casper and according to Blessed Ann Catherine Emmerich his real name is Seir from Kerala, India and Melchoir real name is Mensor from Chaldean, Persia, and Balthasar real name is Theokeno is from Naimans, Mongolia. These three Kings were also astrologers, philosophers, mathematicians, and learned men. These men were following the star of Jacob, predicted in Numbers 24:17 "A star shall come forth out of Jacob, and a scepter shall rise out of Israel." Interesting, these foreigners represent the pagan nations came to "worship" Jesus. These were Middle Eastern, Mid-Asian, and Asian Kings. The Kings with their dromedaries and caravan of nobles, servants and slaves traveled months to visit the birth of Jesus Christ.

Gift to Child Jesus: Matthew writes that the Magi brought three gifts: gold, frankincense, and myrrh. These gifts clearly have deep meanings: the gold represents Jesus' majesty, the frankincense represents His divinity, and the myrrh represents His humanity. Caspar (Seir) is traditionally depicted as the middle of the three kings with a reddish beard, younger than Melchior (Mensor) and older than Balthazar (Theokeno), waiting in line behind Melchior (Mensor) to give the gift of frankincense to the infant Jesus. He is often depicted in the act of receiving gifts from his assistants, or removing his crown, and then representing a sign of readiness to stand at the feet of the infant Jesus Christ.

These Holy Kings, Middle Eastern, Mid-Asian and Asian and entourage, 2000 years ago were all prostrating, adoring, and worshiping our Lord, the Baby Jesus Christ. They were very Blessed to recognize the Son of God. It was not by chance they saw the star which guided them, (please read: The visions of the three Kings leading to an actual coordination and visitation of Jesus). They were also astrologers and they had knowledge of the prophecies that Christ, Son of God was to be born in Bethlehem. They were excited to travel 3 to 4000 miles to see the Son of God, they followed the star which only they could see because they were chosen and they did their work when they went home and talked about their journey and promoted the

Baby Jesus. The Christians of Mensor (Melchoir) from Chaldean (Persia), of Seir (Casper) from Kerala (India), and Theokeno (Balthasar) grew. According to Emmerich that when Jesus was of age He went to visit all three Kings, (please read: Tapestry of Cultures contribute to Jesus' early education).

PRAYER

Epiphany Prayer: Dear Jesus, as You led the Three Kings to You by the light of a star, please draw us ever closer to You by the light of Faith. Help us to desire You as ardently as they did. Give us the grace to overcome all the obstacles that keep us far from You. Amen

O Holy Magi, you were living in continual expectation of the rising of the Star of Jacob, which would announce the birth of the true Son of justice; obtain for me an increase of faith and charity, and the grace to live in continual hope of beholding, one day, the light of heavenly glory and eternal joy.
Amen

O Holy Magi, who at the first appearance of the wondrous star, left your native country to go and seek the new-born King of the Jews; obtain for me the grace of, "Responding promptly, to every Divine inspiration, one day, the light of heavenly glory and eternal joy. Amen

INTRODUCTION

Traditionally, my children and grandchildren look forward to the Three Kings or Three Wise men or Three Magi for one good reason, they are bearing gifts. Actually, there are many more reasons besides bearing gifts. God has a plan. God has especially chosen these Three Kings not only to pay a visit to the birth of His Son, our Lord Jesus Christ, and to let all know they came from Persia, from India and Mongolia, meaning they were Middle Eastern, Middle Asian and Asian. What did they do, they travel months to Bethlehem with their royalties, their servants and their slaves knowing that Baby Jesus was the Son of God. When they arrived, they prostrated, adored and worshipped the Baby Jesus. When they returned to their home land, they continued to promote and evangelize the Son of God.

World's population is 7.9 Billion and Catholic population is 1.4 Billion. Most of today's Catholics do not live in Europe, or the global North. By 2050, 75% of Catholics will live outside the west. **Catholicism, which was born in the Middle East**, is — at least at the grassroots, the Three Kings did their share of evangelization. The share of the world's Catholics who live in Africa has increased from 1.9 million in 1900 to an estimated 236 million today. That's fully 20% of the Church. While the population of Africa increased from 1950 to 2000 by 313%, the Catholic population increased by 708%. In terms of median age, Africa is a young church — and looks to be the center of its future.

Jesus is always "the light of the world" and His Gospel is never to be fully identified with any one culture. However, in order for the Catholic faith to reach hearts and minds, the Gospel needs to be presented in a way to which people can relate.

The Church in Asia, the Asian bishops argued, will only advance if it is Asian in spirit and life. Asian Catholicism will flourish in a threefold encounter, involving sharing life with all of Asia's inhabitants (especially the poor), engaging with local cultures, and dialoguing with Asia's majority faiths of Buddhism, Islam and Hinduism. The proposal of Asian bishops for dialogue suggests patient evangelization through example and cultivating them of the truth of Christianity friendship with people who are religiously different, rather than rushing to convince them of the truth of Christianity. In India, celibacy is not an issue but the relationship of the Christian Gospel to Indian religions is. In many Asian cultures, Catholicism is still widely perceived as foreign and, in some countries such as India and China the Catholic Church is persecuted. Historically, evangelization in Asia has sometimes raised tensions in the Church. The attempts by Jesuits in China and India to create a synthesis between local cultures and Christianity in the 17th and 18th were roundly criticized in Europe and eventually forbidden. of the truth of Christianity. presented in a way to which people can relate. It seems like its time for Our Lord Jesus Christ to renew the Spirit of the Three Holy Kings. Source: USC Dornsife.

DECLARATION

The decree of the Congregation for the Propagation of the Faith, A.A.S. 58, 1186 (approved by Pope Paul Vi on October 14, 1966) states that the Nihil Obstat and Imprimatur are no longer required on publication s that deal with private revelations, provided they contain nothing contrary to faith and morals.

The author wishes to manifest unconditional submission to the final and official judgment of the Magisterium of the Church

ACKNOWLEDGEMENT

Blessed Anne Katherine Emmerich's Visions of the Life of Christ

Her visions, a spiritual treasure for mankind

The story of her visions has come to us thanks to her friend the writer Clemens Brentano and her doctor William Wesener, who transcribed and ordered the detailed explanations that she narrated of her visions. Clemens Brentano was a fiery romantic writer who converted to Catholicism after his contact with Anne Catherine. William Wesener was convinced of the spiritual height of Anne Catherine when she revealed to himself secrets of his personal life that no one could know. In regard to the reason for these visions, Anne Catherine herself refers to us as follows: "Yesterday I fervently asked God to stop giving me these visions, to see me free from the responsibility of referring them. But the Lord did not want to listen to me; rather, I have understood, as I have done on other occasions, that I must refer everything I see, even if they make fun of me and I do not understand the benefit that results from this. I have also known that no one has ever seen these things in the degree and extent to which I see them, and I have understood that they are not my things, but of the Church. "I give you these visions, the Lord told me, not for you, but to be consigned: you must, therefore, communicate them. Now is not the time to work outward wonders. I give you these visions and I have always given them to you, to show that I am with my Church until the end of the centuries.

But the visions, by themselves, do not make anyone blessed: you must exercise, then, charity, patience and all virtues. The admirable visions of the Old Testament and the numerous visions of the lives of saints were communicated to me by the goodness of God, not only for my instruction, but also for me to publish them and make known so many things hidden and ignored. Many times this mandate was instilled in me. I should have died long time ago. I have known through a vision that some time ago I should have died, if it was not for the fact that I had to make these things known through the Pilgrim (that was the name she used to refer affectionately to the writer Clemens Brentano). He must write everything. It is my sole responsibility to communicate my visions. When the Pilgrim has ordered everything and everything is finished, he will die too.

Also my thanks to my proofreader Carol Walsh, my editors and my brother Ralph Khoe and wife Yoka Koo and Father Siby Joseph to and Mike Williams from

Amazon Smart Publishers. Thanks to the Sources which are stated at every related narrative.

DEDICATION TO

Vivek Ramaswamy and Apoorva T Ramaswamy

Other works by the Author

4 Books Compiled and written by Gaby Kool

Three Holy Kings

Super Holy Popes

Holy Kings, Holy Queens, Holy Royalties

Holy Kings, Holy Queens, Holy Royalties Volume II

Table Of Contents

Chapter 1

The Arrival in Bethlehem

Meantime it had grown dark. Mary was standing under the tree, her ungirdled robe falling around her in full folds, her head covered with a white veil. The ass was nearby, its head turned toward the tree, at the foot of which Joseph had made a seat for Mary with the baggage. Crowds were hurrying to and fro in Bethlehem, and many of the passersby gazed curiously at Mary, as one naturally does on seeing a person standing a long time in the dark. I think also that some of them addressed her, and asked her who she was. Ah, they little dreamed that the Saviour was so near! Mary was so patient, so tranquil, so full of hope. Ah, she had indeed long to wait! At last she sat down, her hands crossed on her breast, her head lowered. After a long time, Joseph returned in great dejection. I saw that he was shedding tears and, because he had failed again to find an inn, he hesitated to approach. But suddenly he bethought him of a cave outside Bethlehem used as a storing place by the shepherds when they brought their cattle to the city. Joseph had often withdrawn thither to conceal himself from his brothers and to pray. It was very likely to be deserted at that season or, if any shepherds did come, it would be easy to make friends with them.

He and Mary might there find shelter for awhile, and after a little rest he would go out again on his search. And now they went around to the left, as if through the ruined walls, tombs, and ramparts of a country town. They mounted a rampart or hill, and then the road began again to descend. At last, they reached a hill before which stood trees, firs, pines, or cedars, and trees with small leaves like the box tree. In this hill was the cave or vault spoken of by Joseph. There were no houses around. One side of the cave was built up with rough masonry through which the open entrance of the shepherds led down into the valley. Joseph opened the light wicker door and, as they entered, the she-ass ran to meet them.

The Finding of the Cave

She had left them near Joseph's paternal house, and had run around the city to this cave. She frolicked around and leaped gaily about them, so that Mary said: "Behold! It is surely God's will that we should be here." But Joseph was worried and, in secret, a little ashamed, because he had so often alluded to the good reception they would meet in Bethlehem. There was a projection above the door under which he stationed the ass and then proceeded to arrange a seat for Mary. It was quite dark, about eight o'clock when they reached this place. Joseph struck a light and went into the cave. The entrance was very narrow. The walls were stuffed with all kinds of coarse straw, like rushes, over which hung brown mats.

Back in the vaulted part were some air holes in the roof, but here also everything was in disorder. Joseph cleared it out and prepared as much space in the back part as would afford room for a couch and seat for Mary, who had placed herself on a rug with her bundle for a support. The ass was then brought in, and Joseph fastened a lamp on the wall.

Mary was so patient, so tranquil, so full of hope. Ah, she had indeed long to wait! At last she sat down, her hands crossed on her breast, her head lowered. After a long time, Joseph returned in great dejection. I saw that he was shedding tears and, because he had failed again to find an inn, he hesitated to approach. But suddenly he thought of a cave outside Bethlehem used as a storing place by the shepherds when they brought their cattle to the city. It was very likely to be deserted at that season or, if any shepherds did come, it would be easy to make friends with them. He and Mary might there find shelter for awhile, and after a little rest he would go out again on his search. And now they went around to the left, as if through the ruined walls, tombs, and ramparts of a country town.

While Mary was eating, he went out to the field in the direction of the Milk Cave, and laid a leathern bottle in the rivulet that it might fill. He went also to the city where he procured some little dishes, a bundle of other things, and I think, some fruit. It was, indeed, the Sabbath but, on account of the numerous strangers in the city and their need of various necessaries, provisions and utensils were exposed for sale on tables placed at the street corners. The price was paid down on the spot. I think servants or pagan slaves guarded the tables, but I cannot remember for certain. When Joseph returned, he brought with him a small bundle of slender sticks beautifully bound up with reeds, and a box with a handle in which were glowing coals. These he poured out at the entrance of the cave to make a fire. He next brought the water bottle, which he had filled at the rivulet, and prepared some food. It consisted of a stew, made of yellow corn, some kind of large plant that contained a great many seeds, and a little bread. After they had eaten and Mary had lain down to rest upon her rush couch over which was spread a cover, Joseph began to prepare his own resting place at the entrance of the cave. When this was done, he went again into the city.

Previously to setting out, he had stopped up all the openings of the cave, in order to keep out the air. Then for the first time, I saw the Blessed Virgin on her knees in prayer, after which she lay down upon the carpet on her side, her head resting on her arm, her bundle serving for a pillow. This cave lay at the extremity of the mountain ridge of Bethlehem. A clump of beautiful trees stood in front of the entrance, and thence could be descried some of the towers and roofs of the city. Over the entrance, which was closed by a door made of wickerwork, was a shed. From the door, a moderately wide passage led into the cave, an irregularly formed vault, half-round, half-triangular. On one side of the passage was a recess rather lower than the general surface, and this Joseph had enclosed by curtains for his own sleeping place. The rest of the passage, from the recess to the entrance, he cut off by hangings, and there had a kind of storeroom. The passage was not so lofty as the cave itself, which was vaulted by nature. The inner walls of the cave, where they were formed entirely by nature, though not perfectly even, yet were pleasing and clean; indeed to my eye, there was something about them quite charming. They pleased me more than did those parts upon which some attempts had been made at masonry, for these latter were coarse and rough.

The floor of the cave was deeper than that of the entrance, and was on three sides surrounded by a stone seat somewhat raised, broad in some places, in others narrow. At one of the broad parts, the ass took its stand. It had no trough, but a large leathern bag was placed before it or hung in the corner. Behind was a small side cave just large enough to allow the animal to stand upright. There the fodder was stored. A gutter ran along by this corner, and I saw Joseph cleaning the cave out every day. Where Mary reposed before the birth of the Child and where I beheld her elevated above the ground at the moment of her delivery, there was a similar seat of stone. The spot in which the Crib stood was a deep recess, or side vault. Near it was a second entrance into the cave, which was in the ridge of a hill that ran toward the city. In the rear, the hill sank into a very charming valley planted with rows of trees. This valley led to the Suckling Cave of Abraham, situated in a projection of the opposite hill. The valley may have been one-eighth of an hour in width, and through it flowed that little rivulet from which Joseph had procured the water. Besides the real CribCave, there were in the same hill, but lying somewhat deeper, two other caves, in one of which the Blessed Virgin often remained hidden.

Birth of the Child Jesus

I saw Joseph on the following day arranging a seat and couch for Mary in the so-called Suckling Cave of Abraham, which was also the sepulcher of Maraha, his nurse. It was more spacious than the cave of the Crib. Mary remained there some hours, while Joseph was making the latter more habitable. He brought also from the city many different little vessels and some dried fruits. Mary told him that the birth hour of the Child would arrive on the coming night. It was then nine months since her conception by the Holy Ghost. She begged him to do all in his power that they might receive as honorably as possible this Child promised by God, this Child supernaturally conceived; and she invited him to unite with her in prayer for those hard-hearted people who would afford Him no place of shelter. Joseph proposed to bring some pious women whom he knew in Bethlehem to her assistance; **but Mary would not allow it**, she declared that she had no need of anyone. It was five o'clock in the evening when Joseph brought Mary back again to the Crib Cave.

He hung up several more lamps, and made a place under the shed before the door for the little she-ass, which came joyfully hurrying from the fields to meet them. When Mary told Joseph that her time was drawing near and that he should now betake himself to prayer, he left her and turned toward his sleeping place to do her bidding. Before entering his little recess, he looked back once toward that part of the cave where Mary knelt upon her couch in prayer, her back to him, her face toward the east. He saw the cave filled with the light that streamed from Mary, for she was entirely enveloped as if by flames. It was as if he were, like Moses, looking into the burning bush. He sank prostrate to the ground in prayer, and looked not back again. The glory around Mary became brighter and brighter, the lamps that Joseph had lit were no longer to be seen. Mary knelt, her flowing white robe spread out before her. At the twelfth hour, her prayer became ecstatic, **and I saw her raised so far above the ground** that one could see it beneath her. Her hands were crossed upon her breast, and the light around her grew even more resplendent. I no longer saw the roof of the cave.

Above Mary stretched a pathway of light up to Heaven, in which pathway it seemed as if one light came forth from another, as if one figure dissolved into another, and from these different spheres of light other heavenly figures issued. Mary continued in prayer, her eyes bent low upon the ground. **At that moment she gave birth to the Infant Jesus. I saw Him like a tiny, shining Child, lying on the rug at her knees, and brighter far than all the other brilliancy.** He seemed to grow before my eyes. But dazzled by the glittering and flashing of light, I know not whether I really saw that, or how I saw it. Even inanimate nature seemed stirred. The stones of the rocky floor and the walls of the cave were glimmer ingand sparkling, as if instinct with life. Mary's ecstasy lasted some moments longer. Then I saw her spread a cover over the Child, but she did not yet take Him up, nor even touch Him. After a long time, I saw the Child stirring and heard Him crying, and then only did Mary seem to recover full consciousness. She lifted the Child, along with the cover that she had thrown over it, to her breast and sat veiled, herself and Child quite enveloped. I think she was suckling Him. **I saw angels around her in human form prostrate on their faces.**

It may, perhaps, have been an hour after the birth when Mary called St. Joseph, who still lay prostrate in prayer. When he approached, he fell on his knees, his face to the ground, in a transport of joy, devotion, and humility. **Mary again urged him to look upon the Sacred Gift from Heaven, and then did Joseph take the Child into his arms.** And now the Blessed Virgin swathed the Child in red and over that in a white veil up as far as under the little arms, and the upper part of the body from the armpits to the head, she wrapped up in another piece of linen. She had only four swaddling cloths with her. She laid the Child in the Crib, which had been filled with rushes and fine moss over which was spread a cover that hung down at the sides. The Crib stood over the stone trough, and at this spot the ground stretched straight and level as far as the passage, where it made a broader flexure toward the south. The floor of this part of the cave lay somewhat deeper than where the Child was born, and down to it steps had been formed in the earth. When Mary laid the Child in the Crib, both she and Joseph stood by Him in tears, singing the praises of God.

The seat and the couch of the Blessed Virgin were near the Crib. I saw her on the first day sitting upright and also resting on her side, though I noticed in her no special signs of weakness or sickness. Both before and after the birth, she was robed in white. When visitors came, she generally sat near the Crib more closely veiled. On the night of the Birth there gushed forth a beautiful spring in the other cave that lay to the right. The water ran out, and the next day Joseph dug a course for it and formed a spring. In those visions to which the event itself, and not the feast of the Church, gave rise, I saw, indeed, no such sparkling joy in nature as I sometimes see at holy Christmastide. Then the joy has an interior signification. But yet, I saw extraordinary gladness, and in many places, even in the most distant regions of the world, something marvelous on that midnight. By it the good were filled with joyful longings, and the bad with dread. I saw also many of the lower animals joyfully agitated. I saw fountains gushing forth and swelling, flowers springing up in many places, trees and plants budding with new life, and all sending forth their fragrance.

Angels were singing

In Bethlehem it was misty, and the sky above shone with a murky, reddish glare. But over the valley of the shepherds, around the Crib, and in the vale of the Suckling Cave floated bright cloud so freshing dew. I saw the herds of the three oldest shepherds near the hill under sheds; but those further on near the shepherds' tower, were partly in the open air. The three eldest shepherds, roused by the wonders of the night, I saw standing together before their huts, gazing around and pointing out the magnificent light that shone over the Crib. The shepherds at the distant tower were also in full movement. They had climbed up the tower and were looking toward the Crib over which they, too, saw the light. I saw something like a cloud of glory descend upon the three shepherds. I saw in it figures moving to and fro, and heard the approach of sweet, clear voices singing softly. At first, the shepherds were frightened. Soon there stood before them five or seven lovely, radiant figures holding in their hands a long strip like a scroll upon which were written words in letters a hand in length. The angels were singing. The angels appeared also to the shepherds on the tower and where else, I do not now recall. I did not see them hurrying off at once to the cave. The first three were indeed an hour and a half distant from it, and those on the tower as far again. But I saw that they began at once to reflect upon what gifts they should take to the newborn Saviour, and to get them together as quickly as possible. The three shepherds went to the Crib early next morning. I saw that Anne at Nazareth (Mother of Mary), Elizabeth in Juttah, Noemi, Anna, and Simeon in the Temple—all had on this night visions from which they learned the birth of the Saviour. The child John was unspeakably joyous. But only Anne knew where the newborn Child was; the others, and even Elizabeth, knew indeed of Mary and saw her in vision, but they knew nothing of Bethlehem. I saw something very wonderful taking place in the Temple. The writings of the Sadducees were more than once hurled by an invisible force from the places in which they were kept, which circumstance gave rise to unaccountable dread. The fact was ascribed to sorcery, and large sums of money were paid to hush the matter up.

I saw that in Rome, across the river where numbers of Jews dwelt, a well of oil gushed forth spontaneously, to the wonder of all the witnesses. And when Jesus was born, a magnificent statue of the god Jupiter fell with violence from its place. All were struck with fear. Sacrifices were offered and another idol, I think Venus, was interrogated as to the cause. The devil was forced to speak by its mouth, and he proclaimed that it had happened because a virgin unmarried had conceived and brought forth a son. He told them also of the miracle of the oil well. Where this took place now stands a church in honor of the Mother of God. I saw that the pagan priests were deeply perplexed at the whole affair. They searched their writings, and discovered the following history.

Pious Woman Prophesy

About seventy years previously, this idol (Jupiter) had been greatly venerated. It was magnificently ornamented with gold and precious stones, grand ceremonies were held in its honor, and numerous sacrifices offered to it. But there was in Rome at that time an extraordinarily pious woman who lived on her own means. I know not for certain whether she was a Jewess or not; but she had visions, uttered prophecies, and informed many persons as to the cause of their sterility. This woman had thrown out words to this effect that they should not honor the idol at so great a cost, for that they would one day behold it burst asunder in their midst. This speech proved so offensive that she was imprisoned and tormented until by her prayers she obtained from God the information as to when that misfortune would happen. The pagan priests demanded what had been revealed to her, and when at last she replied: "The idol will be shattered when an Immaculate Virgin shall bring forth a son," they hooted at her, and released her as a fool. And now the people recalled the fact and declared that the woman had spoken truly. I saw also that the Roman consuls, of whom one was named Lentulus and who was a friend of St. Peter and an ancestor of the martyr-priest Moses, made notes of this occurrence, as well as that of the bursting forth of the oil well.

Emperor Augustus apparition of a rainbow upon which sat the Virgin and Child

On this night, I saw the Emperor Augustus at the Capitol where he had an apparition of a rainbow upon which sat the Virgin and Child. From the oracle that he caused to be interrogated upon what he had seen, he received the answer: "A Child is born, and before Him we must all flee!" The emperor at once erected an altar and offered sacrifice to the Son of the Virgin, as to the "Firstborn of God." I had also a vision of Egypt far beyond Matarea, Heliopolis, and Memphis. There was in that region a large idol that used to give answers to all kinds of questions. Suddenly it became mute. The king ordered immense sacrifices to be offered throughout his whole dominions. Then was the devil, upon the command of God, forced to say: "I have become silent, I must give place to another. The Son of the Virgin is born, and a temple will be here erected to His honor." Upon hearing this, the king wanted to raise a temple to the newborn Child next to that of the god, but I do not clearly recall the story. I know, however, that the idol was put aside and that a temple was erected to the Virgin and Child whom it had proclaimed, and who were afterward honored with pagan rites. The visions of the three Kings leading to an actual coordination and visitation of Jesus I beheld a great wonder in the country of the Three Kings. There was a tower on a mountain to which the Kings retired in turn with a retinue of priests, in order to observe the stars. What they saw they committed to writing and communicated to one another. On this night there were two of them there, Mensor and Seir. The third, who dwelt toward the east side of the Caspian Sea (most probable Naimans, Mongolis)), was called Theokeno. He was not present. There was a certain constellation at which they always gazed, and whose variations they noted. In it they saw visions and pictures. Upon this night also, they had several visions of various kinds.

It was not in one star alone that they saw those visions, but in several that formed a figure, and there seemed to be a movement in them. They saw the vision of the moon over which arose a beautiful rainbow-colored arch on which was seated a Virgin. The left limb was drawn up in a sitting posture, the right hung a little lower and rested on the moon. To the left of the Virgin and rising above the arch, was a grapevine, and on her right a sheaf of wheat. In front of the Virgin was a chalice like that used at the Last Supper. It appeared to issue, but with greater clearness and brightness, from the brilliancy that emanated from her. Out of the chalice arose a Child, and over the Child shone a bright disk like an empty ostensorium. It was surrounded by radiating beams. It reminded me of the Blessed Sacrament. On the Virgin's right was an octangular church with a golden door and two small side-doors. With the right hand, the Virgin put the Child and the host into the church which, meanwhile, grew larger and larger, and in which I saw the Most Holy Trinity. Above the church arose a tower. Theokeno, the third king, had similar visions in his own home.

Over the head of the Virgin sitting on the arch shone a star, which suddenly shot from its place and skimmed along the heavens before the Kings. It was for them a voice announcing as never before that the Child, so long awaited by them and by their ancestors, was at last born in Judea, and that they were to follow that star. For some nights immediately preceding that blessed one, they had from their tower seen all kinds of visions in the heavens, kings journeying to the Child and offering their homage to the Child. So now they hurriedly gathered together their treasures and with gifts and presents began the journey, for they did not want to be the last. For they do want to miss the boat that has shone to them in a very vivid supernatural way to the King of the Universe. I saw all three after a few days meeting on the way.

Knowledge of One God:

Emperor Shun (2230 B.C.) believed in one God called Shangdi who was the supreme ruler of the universe. Shangdi means "Emperor", "Supreme Deity" or "Highest

Deity". Shangdi was never made into an idol or image. The Emperor functioned not only as ruler but also as high priest. The Shu Jing depicts Emperor Shun making the annual sacrifice to Shangdi. Sacrifices were made in the Temple of Heaven which contained Shangdi's throne. A completely healthy bull would be sacrificed by the emperor and a tablet with Shangdi's name inscribed on it would be placed on the throne at the north end of the Temple of Heaven. The ancient ceremony that the Emperor performed while sacrificing the bull began with: "Of old in the beginning, there was the great chaos, without form and dark. The five elements [planets] had not begun to revolve, nor the sun and the moon to shine. In the midst thereof there existed neither forms for sound. Thou, O spiritual Sovereign, camest forth in Thy presidency, and first didst divide the grosser parts from the purer. Thou madest heaven; Thou madest earth; Thou madest man. All things with their reproductive power got their being. "This sounds quite similar to Genesis 1:1-2 "In the beginning God created the heavens and the earth.

The earth was without form and void, and darkness was upon the face of the deep".The ceremony continued with "Thou regardest us as a Father" and ended with: "Thy sovereign goodness is infinite. As a potter, Thou hast made all living things. Thy sovereign goodness is infinite. Great and small are sheltered [by Thee]. As engraven on the heart of Thy poor servant is the sense of Thy goodness, so that my feeling cannot be fully displayed. With great kindness Thou dost bear us, and not withstanding our shortcomings, dost grant us life and prosperity." Once again we see a similarity to Isaiah 64:8, "But now, O Lord, Thou art our Father; we are the clay, and Thou our Potter and we all are the work of Thy hand".

China had a revelation of who God was that had been passed down to them from generation to generation. It is clear that Noah shared his knowledge of God with his descendants. Later other deities and ancestral worship were added in addition to Shangdi, but China began as a monotheistic people. Today, Shangdi is considered the God of the Christians in China, Hong Kong, and Taiwan.

Christ is Coming

Let's fast forward 2,000 years. Wise men from the east come looking for Jesus. How in the world did they know this? There came wise men from the east to Jerusalem, saying, "Where is he that is born King of the Jews? for we have seen his star in the east, and are come to worship him." Matthew 2:1-2An explanation as to who these wise men were and where they came from can be explained by the record of the Chinese emperor Jianping (3 B.C. – 6 B.C.): "In the second month of the second year, the comet was out of Altair for more than 70 days…It is said, ‘Comets appear to signify the old being replaced by the new.’ Altair, the sun, the moon and the five stars are in movement to signify the beginning of a new epoch; The beginning of a new year, a new month and a new day…The appearance of this comet undoubtedly symbolizes change. The extended appearance of this comet indicates that this is of great importance.”

Taken from Astronomy Records of the Book of the Han Dynasty.

Most Christian scholars agree that Jesus was born somewhere between 5-6 B.C. Emperor Jianping clearly recognized that the star Altair signified something very significant. Altair is one of the brightest stars in the Chinese sky. Altair was observed for about 70 days. Seventy days is the estimated amount of travel time needed to get from China to Israel. What made Emperor Jianping realize the star’s appearance was important? “The primary meaning of Altair, the key supporting pillar of the heavens, is the Perfect Sacrifice.” Historical records, Vol. 27, Book of Astronomy.

Altair is in the constellation Aquila. In Chinese Aquila means “the heaven eagle constellation”. Chinese astronomers and emperors interpreted this information to mean that a king was coming and that He was worthy of worship. Possibly, they believed that Shangdi was coming for the throne that they had constructed for Him in the Temple of Heaven. Emperor Guang Wu reigned during the time of Christ’s death and resurrection. The fact that he and astronomers knew Christ was God is shown in Chinese historical records dated around A.D 31. “Yin and Yang have mistakenly switched, and the sun and moon were eclipsed. The sins of all the people are now on one man. Pardon is proclaimed to all under heaven.” History of Latter Han Dynasty, Volume 1, Chronicles of Emperor Guang Wu, 7th year. “In the day of Gui Hai, the last day of the month, there was a solar eclipse. [The emperor] avoided the Throne Room, suspended all military activities and did not handle official business for five days.” History of Latter Han Dynasty, Vol. 1, Chronicles of Emperor Guang Wu, 7th year”.

Another historical record says:

“Eclipse on the day of Gui Hai, Man from Heaven died”. History of Latter Han, Annals, No. 18, Gui Hai. As we know, when Christ died there was darkness that covered the earth. “From the sixth hour until the ninth hour darkness came over all the land.” Mark 15:33. Three days after the eclipse this was recorded by Chinese astronomers: “During the reign of Emperor Guang Wu, on the day of Bing Yin of the fourth month of Jian Wu, a halo–a rainbow–encircled the sun." History of Latter Han, Annals No. 18, Gui Hai. Christ's resurrection also apparently caused a celestial event that was observable. It is clear that Christ did not hide Himself from the Chinese people. I always found it odd that the far east is never mentioned in the New Testament. The Holy Spirit sent Paul and the apostles of His church throughout the ancient world to preach the Gospel, yet it always seemed that ancient China was overlooked. It was never overlooked. God knew that the Chinese people already saw the signs in the heavens. The Chinese people recognized the King was born before the people of Israel did. They mourned His death when others were cheering. They recognized that something miraculous was occurring on the earth before it had ever been made public. God is not confined to our knowledge or our understanding of how He works. God has been revealing Himself for generations to the generations and He will continue to do so.

Adoration of the Shepherds. Devout Visits to the Crib

In the early dawn after the birth of Jesus, the three oldest of the shepherds came to the Crib Cave with the gifts they had gathered together. These consisted of little animals bearing some resemblance to deer. They were very lightly built and nimble, had long necks and clear, beautiful eyes. They followed or ran along beside the shepherds who led them with fine, guiding cords. The shepherds carried also large, live birds under their arms, and dead ones slung over their shoulders. They told Joseph at the entrance of the cave what the angel had announced to them, and that they had come to do homage to the Child of Promise and to offer Him gifts. Joseph accepted their presents and allowed them to lead the animals into the space that formed a kind of cellar near the side entrance of the cave. Then he conducted them to the Blessed Virgin, who was sitting on the ground near the Crib, a rug under her, the Infant Jesus on her lap. The shepherds, their staves resting on their arms, fell on their knees and wept with joy. They knelt long, tasting great interior sweetness, and then intoned the angelic canticle of praise, and a Psalm that I have forgotten. When they were about to take leave, Mary placed the Child in their arms. Some of the other shepherds came in the evening, accompanied by women and children, and bringing gifts. They sang most sweetly before the Crib the same Psalms, and short refrains of which I remember the words: "O Child, blooming as a rose art Thou! As a herald Thou comest forth!" They brought gifts of birds, eggs, honey, woven stuffs of various colors, bundles of raw silk, and ears of corn, also several bundles of a corn with heavy grains growing on a stalk with large leaves like those of rushes.

Cave of the Nativity, Bethlehem

The site of the Nativity is attested to by an unbroken tradition dating back to the 2nd Century. This plan is a suggested reconstruction of the original arrangement based on the description in the "and the present form of the caves (shaded areas). During the centuries there have been many additions and enlargements. Sister Emmerich stated that new grottoes were cut in the rock even during the lifetime of Our Lord. The basilica (Saint Mary Major Cathedral), erected by Constantine over the cave in the 4th Century, and still in use, is one of the oldest Christian churches in the world). The three oldest shepherds came back in turn and helped Joseph to make the Crib Cave and its surroundings more comfortable. I saw also several pious women with the Blessed Virgin, performing some services for her. They were Essenians, and lived in the valley, not far from the Crib Cave, in little rocky cells adjoining one another. They owned little gardens near their cells, and they taught the children of their community. St. Joseph had invited them to come, for he was acquainted with them even in early youth. He visited these pious women who dwelt in the side of the rock. They now came in turn to the Blessed Virgin, bringing little necessaries and bundles of wood. They cooked and washed for the Holy Family.

Some days after the birth of Jesus, I saw a touching scene in the Crib Cave. Joseph and Mary were standing by the Crib and gazing with emotion upon the Infant Jesus, when suddenly the ass fell upon its knees and lowered its head to the ground. Mary and Joseph shed tears. I saw Mary at another time standing by the Crib. As she gazed upon the Child, the deep conviction stole upon her that Him had come upon earth to suffer. That reminded me of a vision I had had at an earlier period in which I had been shown how Jesus, while still in His Mother's womb and from the moment of His birth, had suffered. I saw under the heart of Mary a glory and in it a bright shining Child. As I gazed upon It, it seemed as if Mary were hovering over Him and surrounding Him. I beheld the Child growing and all the torments of the Crucifixion inflicted upon Him. It was a sad, a fearful sight! I wept and sobbed aloud. I saw other forms around Him beating and pushing, scourging and crowning Him. Then they laid the Cross upon Him, next nailed Him to the same, and pierced Him in the side. I saw the whole Passion of Christ in the Child. It was a frightful sight! As the Child hung on the Cross, He said to me: "All this did I suffer from My conception until My thirty-fourth year, when My Passion was outwardly consummated." (The Lord died when He was thirty-three years and three months old.) "Go and announce it to men!" But how can I announce it to men?

I saw Jesus also as the newborn Child, and I saw how many of the children that went to the Crib ill treated the Infant Jesus. The Mother of God was not there to protect the Child, and the children went with all kinds of switches and rods, and struck Him in the face until the Blood flowed. The Child meekly extended His little hands before His face, in order to ward off the blows. The smallest children were they that struck the most maliciously. The parents of some even twisted and wrapped the rods for them. They brought thorns, nettles, whips, little rods of all kinds, each having its own signification. One came with a very slender rod, like a reed. But when it was about to strike the Child, the rod snapped, and fell back upon itself. I knew several of the children. Some went about boasting in their fine clothes, but I stripped them, and whipped some of them well.

While Mary was still standing by the Crib in deep meditation, some shepherds drew near with their wives, in all about five persons. To give them room to approach the Crib, the Blessed Virgin withdrew a little to the spot upon which she had given birth to the Child. The people did not actually adore, but they gazed down upon the Child deeply moved, and before leaving they bowed low over Him as if kissing Him. It was day. Mary sat in her usual place with the Infant Jesus on her lap. He was swathed, the hands and face alone free, Mary had something like a piece of linen in her hands with which she was busied. Joseph was at the fireplace near the entrance of the cave, and appeared to be making a shelf to hold some vessels. I was standing next the ass. And now came in three aged female Essenians, who were cordially welcomed, though Mary did not rise. They brought quite a number of presents: small fruits, birds with red, awl-shaped beaks as large as ducks, which they carried by the wings, oval rolls about an inch in thickness, some linen, and other stuff. All were received with rare humility and gratitude. The women were very silent and recollected. Deeply moved, they gazed down upon the Child, but they did not touch Him. When they withdrew, it was without farewells or ceremony. Meanwhile, I was taking a good look at the ass. It had a very broad back, and I thought to myself: "You good beast! You have carried a great burden!" and I wanted to feel it, to see if it were real. I ran my hand over its hair, and it felt as smooth as silk.

Now came two married women with three little girls about eight years old. They appeared to be strangers and people of distinction, who had come in obedience to a call more miraculous than that received by any previous visitor. Joseph welcomed them very humbly. They brought presents less in size than the others, but of greater value: grain in a bowl, small fruits, and a cluster of thick, triangular, gold leaves on which was a stamp like a seal. I thought: "Strange! That looks like the representation of the eye of God! But no! How can I compare the eye of God with red earth!" Mary arose and placed the Child in the ladies' arms. Both held Him a little while, praying silently with uplifted heart, and then kissed Him. The three little girls were silent and deeply impressed. Joseph and Mary conversed with their visitors and when they left,

Joseph accompanied them part of the way. Ah! Could we, like these women, behold the beauty, the purity, the innocent wisdom of Mary! She knew all things! But in her humility, she appears unconscious of her gifts. Like a child, she casts down her eyes; and when she raises them, her glance, like a flash of lightning, like the truth, like a ray of unsullied light, pierces one through and through. That is because she is perfectly pure, perfectly innocent, full of the Holy Ghost, and without any reflection on self. No one can resist her glance.

Jesus and the Essenes (explanation of the Essenes)

In 2020, Meru University offered an exciting course on the relationship between Jesus and a little-known Jewish community called the Essenes. For many Meru University students who had never heard of the Essenes, the course proved to be an eye-opening education. Using scholarly resources released in the 20th century, David Christopher Lewis presented a fascinating account of the childhood education of Jesus of Nazareth by this Jewish sect. Historical records have recently come to light, compelling us to acknowledge the influence the Essene Community had upon the life and ministry of Jesus.

Weaving diverse and independent sources that confirm the existence of the Essenes at the time of Jesus' birth, we understand with greater insight the rich cultural milieu and wide spectrum of religious and spiritual teachings to which the boy Jesus, spoken of as *Yeshua* in their texts, had access. Who was this secretive and remotely situated community of Jews who dedicated their lives to the preservation of the holy books of the law, the sacred Torah, and to its author, the God they worshiped as Jehovah, or *Yahweh*?

Referred to by some researchers as the "people of the covenant" or the "covenanters," we learn that the Essenes, inhabitants of these far-flung desert dwellings in and around ancient Palestine, dedicated their lives to a singular purpose.[1.] The main objective of the several redoubts maintained by the Essenes was the accumulation, preservation and ultimate dissemination of the sacred knowledge that lay at the very foundation of what the Christian world refers to as the Old Testament books of the Bible. We now know that these desert dwellers were keeping the vigil for the coming of a Messiah, whose prophetic arrival in their lifetime was a subject of recurring scholastic scrutiny. When that much-anticipated time should arrive, the Essenes were prepared to welcome and support the mission of this great soul whom many today call Savior.

Source: David Christopher Lewis

Tapestry of Cultures Contribute to Jesus' Early Education

Not many Christians realize that the boy Jesus had a wealthy uncle, Joseph of Arimathea. A merchant who owned a sizable fleet of ships, he plied the trade routes and very nearly controlled a monopoly in the trading of tin, which he sourced from the rich mines located in Cornwall, England. Tin was a very prized metal in that era in that it alloys with copper to form bronze weapons and implements. Accompanying him on several voyages was his young nephew Jesus. Now with insights afforded us by the Essene teachings, along with other corroborating evidence, it is apparent that Joseph was well aware of the singular destiny that awaited his gifted nephew. So, it is not too far-fetched to read that Jesus had the opportunity to study under master teachers in universities of the Druids, while accompanying his uncle Josephius to England. What's more, due to the patronage of his uncle, Jesus traveled all over the known world. His travels took him to the Orient to learn from the lamas of Tibet, and he studied with Hindu Brahmins, Egyptian high priests, and Jewish Kabbalist scholars.

Source: The Heart Center

The Circumcision

Joseph returned from Bethlehem with five priests and a woman whose services were necessary on such occasions. They brought with them the circumcision stool and an octangular slab with all that was needed for the ceremony. All this was placed in order in the passage. The stool was hollow and formed a chest, which could be taken apart, thus affording a kind of low seat with a support on the side. It was covered with red. The circumcision stone was, perhaps, over two feet in diameter. In the center was a metal plate under which, in a hollow of the stone, were all kinds of little boxes containing fluids. These boxes were in separate compartments, and at one side lay the circumcision knife. The stone was laid upon the little stool which, covered with a cloth, always stood on the spot upon which Jesus was born, and the circumcision stool was placed next to it. That evening a repast was spread under the arbor at the entrance to the cave. A crowd of poor people had followed the priests, as is usual on such occasions, and during the meal they were continually receiving something both from the priests and from Joseph. The priests went to Mary and the Child, spoke with the mother, and took the Child in their arms. They also spoke to Joseph about the name the Child was to receive. They prayed and sang the greater part of the night, and circumcised the Child at daybreak.

Mary was very much troubled, very anxious about It. After the ceremony, the Infant Jesus was swathed in red and white as far as under the little arms, which also were bound and the head wrapped in a cloth. The Child was again laid on the octangular stone, and prayers recited over It. If I remember rightly, the angel had already told Joseph that the Child should be called Jesus, and I have a faint recollection that one of the priests did not at first approve the name, consequently, they still continued in prayer. Then I saw a radiant angel stand-ing in front of the priest and holding before him a tablet like that above the Cross, upon which was inscribed the name of Jesus. I saw the priest writing the name upon a scrap of parchment. I know not whether he or any of the others saw the angel, but deeply moved, he wrote the name under divine inspiration. After that, Joseph received the Child back and handed It to the Blessed Virgin who, with two other women, was standing back in the Crib Cave. Mary took the weeping Child into her arms and quieted It. Some shepherds were standing at the entrance of the cave. Lamps were burning, and the dawn was breaking.

There was some more praying and singing and, before the priests departed, they took a little breakfast. I saw that all present at the circumcision were good people. The priests were enlightened and later attained salvation. Alms were distributed the whole morning to many poor people who presented themselves. Afterward followed a crowd of beggars, filthy, black creatures, very repulsive to me. They carried bundles and, coming up from the valley of the shepherds, passed the Crib as if going to Jerusalem for the celebration of a feast. They were very boisterous, cursing and scolding horribly, because they did not receive by way of alms, as much as they wanted. I do not know exactly what was the matter with them. During the ceremony of circumcision, the ass was tied further back than usual; at other times, it stood in the Crib Cave.

During the day, I saw the nurse again with Mary attending to the Child. That night, the Child was very restless from pain. It cried, and Mary and Joseph tried to soothe Him by carrying Him up and down the cave. While reflecting upon the mystery of the circumcision, I had a vision. I saw two angels with little tablets in their hands, standing under a palm tree. Upon one tablet were pictured various instruments of martyrdom, of which I remember one, a pillar which stood in the middle. On it was a mortar, which had two rings. On the other tablet were letters denoting the seasons and years of the Church. On the palm tree and as if growing out of it, was kneeling a Virgin, her flowing mantle, or veil, for it was fastened over her head, floating around her. In her hands was a heart upon which I saw a tiny, shining Child. I saw an apparition of God the Father draw near to the palm tree, break off a heavy branch that formed a cross, and lay it on the Child. Then I saw the Child raised, as it were, on the cross, and the Virgin reaching the palm branch with the crucified Child on it to God the Father, the heart alone remaining in her hand.

About the name the Child was to receive. They prayed and sang the greater part of the night, and circumcised the Child at daybreak. Mary was very much troubled, very anxious about It. After the ceremony, the Infant Jesus was swathed in red and white as far as under the little arms, which also were bound and the head wrapped in a cloth. The Child was again laid on the octangular stone, and prayers recited over Him. If I remember rightly, the angel had already told Joseph that the Child should be called Jesus, and I have a faint recollection that one of the priests did not at first approve the name, consequently, they still continued in prayer. Then I saw a radiant angel standing in front of the priest and holding before him a tablet like that above the Cross, upon which was inscribed the name of Jesus. I saw the priest writing the name upon a scrap of parchment. I know not whether he or any of the others saw the angel, but deeply moved, he wrote the name under divine inspiration. After that, Joseph received the Child back and handed Him to the Blessed Virgin who, with two other women, was standing back in the Crib Cave.

Mary took the weeping Child into her arms and quieted Him. Some shepherds were standing at the entrance of the cave. Lamps were burning, and the dawn was breaking. There was some more praying and singing and, before the priests departed, they took a little breakfast. I saw that all present at the circumcision were good people. The priests were enlightened and later attained salvation. Alms were distributed the whole morning to many poor people who presented themselves. Afterward followed a crowd of beggars, filthy, black creatures, very repulsive to me. They carried bundles and, coming up from the valley of the shepherds, passed the Crib as if going to Jerusalem for the celebration of a feast. They were very boisterous, cursing and scolding horribly, because they did not receive by way of alms, as much as they wanted. I do not know exactly what was the matter with them. During the ceremony of circumcision, the ass was tied further back than usual; at other times, it stood in the Crib Cave.

During the day, I saw the nurse again with Mary attending to the Child. That night, the Child was very restless from pain. It cried, and Mary and Joseph tried to soothe Him by carrying Him up and down the cave. While reflecting upon the mystery of the circumcision, I had a vision. I saw two angels with little tablets in their hands, standing under a palm tree.

Upon one tablet were pictured various instruments of martyrd**om, of which I remember one, a pillar which stood in the middle. On it was a mortar, which**

had two rings. On the other tablet were letters denoting the seasons and years of the Church. On the palm tree and as if growing out of it, was kneeling a Virgin, her flowing mantle, or veil, for it was fastened over her head, floating around her. In her hands was a heart upon which I saw a tiny, shining Child. I saw an apparition of God the Father draw near to the palm tree, break off a heavy branch that formed a cross, and lay it on the Child. Then I saw the Child raised, as it were, on the cross, and the Virgin reaching the palm branch with the crucified Child on it to God the Father, the heart alone remaining in her hand.

On the evening of the following day, I saw Elizabeth on an ass and accompanied by an old servant, coming from Juta to the cave. Joseph received her most cordially. The joy of Mary and Elizabeth was extremely great as they embraced each other. Elizabeth pressed the Child to her heart. She slept in Mary's cave next the place in which Jesus was born. Before the sacred spot stood a stool upon which they often laid the Child. Mary told Elizabeth all that had happened to her, and when Elizabeth heard of their difficulty in getting a lodging on their arrival in Bethlehem, she wept heartily. Mary gave her all the details of the Infant Jesus' birth. I remember hearing her say that she had been in ecstasy ten minutes at the time of the Annunciation, that it appeared to her as if her heart had grown double its size and that she was filled with unspeakable happiness. But at the Child's birth she had experienced an intense longing. She felt while kneeling that she was upheld by angels, and as if her heart was broken asunder and one-half taken from her. She had also been ten minutes in ecstasy at the time of the birth. She had been conscious of an emptiness within her, a longing after something outside of herself.

Suddenly a light shone before her, and the figure of the Child seemed to grow before her eyes. Then she saw Him moving and heard Him crying and, coming to herself, she raised Him from the rug to her breast, for at first seeing He environed with glory, she had hesitated to take Him up. Elizabeth said: "Thou hast not given birth in the same way as other mothers. The birth of John was sweet also, but it was not like that of thy Child." Once I saw Elizabeth with Mary and the Child concealing themselves toward evening in the side cave. They remained there the whole night, for visitors from Bethlehem were approaching by whom they did not want to be seen. The Jewish women do not leave their children long without other nourishment than the breast; and so the Infant Jesus was fed in those first days on pap made of the sweet, light, nutritious pith of a certain rush-like plant. As in the Temple at Jerusalem, the holy Feast of the Machabees began at this time, it was also celebrated by Joseph in the Crib Cave. He fastened three lamps with seven little lights on the walls of the cave and, during a whole week, lighted them morning and evening. Once I saw in the cave one of the priests who had been present at the Child's circumcision. He had a roll of writings from which he prayed with St. Joseph. It seemed to me that he wanted to find out whether Joseph kept that feast or not. I think, too, that he announced to him another, for a fast-day was near at hand. I saw the preparations for it in Jerusalem. Food was prepared the day before the feast, the fire was covered, servile work was put aside, the doors and windows were hung with tapestry.

Anne often sent servants with gifts of provisions and utensils, all of which Mary soon distributed to the poor. Once Anne sent a beautiful little basket of fruit with large, newly-blown roses stuck in among it. The pink roses were paler than ours, almost flesh colored, and there were some yellow, and some white. Mary was very much pleased, and placed it beside her. And now came Anne herself, accompanied by her second husband and a servant. The Infant Jesus stretched out His little arms to her, and great was her joyful emotion. Mary gave her a full account of all as she had done to Elizabeth. They mingled their tears together, pausing at times to fondle the Infant Jesus. Anne had brought with her many things for Mary and the Child, coverlets, swathing-bands, etc. Although Mary had already received so many things from her, yet the Crib Cave was still quite poor in appearance, since whatever was at all unnecessary was given away at once. Mary told Anne that the Kings from the East were approaching with rich gifts, and that their coming would attract much attention. Anne, therefore, resolved to go and stay with her sister, who dwelt at some hours' distance, and to return after the departure of the royal visitors. Then I saw Joseph set to work to clear out the Crib Cave as well as those in its vicinity, in order to prepare for the arrival of the Kings whom Mary in spirit had seen coming. He went also to Bethlehem to make the second payment of taxes and to look around for a dwelling, for he intended to settle in Bethlehem after Mary's Purification.

The visions of the three Kings leading to an actual coordination and visitation of Jesus I beheld a great wonder in the country of the Three Kings. There was a tower on a mountain to which the Kings retired in turn with a retinue of priests, in order to observe the stars. What they saw they committed to writing and communicated to one another. On this night there were two of them there, Mensor and Seir. The third, who dwelt toward the east side of the Caspian Sea (most probable Naimans, Mongolis)), was called Theokeno. He was not present. There was a certain constellation at which they always gazed, and whose variations they noted. In it they saw visions and pictures. Upon this night also, they had several visions of various kinds. It was not in one star alone that they saw those visions, but in several that formed a figure, and there seemed to be a movement in them. They saw the vision of the moon over which arose a beautiful rainbow-colored arch on which was seated a Virgin. The left limb was drawn up in a sitting posture, the right hung a little lower and rested on the moon. To the left of the Virgin and rising above the arch, was a grapevine, and on her right a sheaf of wheat. In front of the Virgin was a chalice like that used at the Last Supper.

It appeared to issue, but with greater clearness and brightness, from the brilliancy that emanated from her. Out of the chalice arose a Child, and over the Child shone a bright disk like an empty ostensorium. It was surrounded by radiating beams. It reminded me of the Blessed Sacrament. On the Virgin's right was an octangular church with a golden door and two small side-doors. With the right hand, the Virgin put the Child and the host into the church which, meanwhile, grew larger and larger, and in which I saw the Most Holy Trinity. Above the church arose a tower. Theokeno, the third king, had similar visions in his own home. Over the head of the Virgin sitting on the arch shone a star, which suddenly shot from its place and skimmed along the heavens before the Kings. It was for them a voice announcing as never before that the Child, so long awaited by them and by their ancestors, was at last born in Judea, and that they were to follow that star. For some nights immediately preceding that blessed one, they had from their tower seen all kinds of visions in the heavens, kings journeying to the Child and offering their homage to It. So now they hurriedly gathered together their treasures and with gifts and presents began the journey, for they did not want to be the last. For they do want to miss the boat that has shone to them in a very vivid supernatural way to the King of the Universe. I saw all three after a few days meeting on the way.

Chapter 2

The coming of the Three Holy Kings

Emperor Augustus apparition of a rainbow upon which sat the Virgin and Child

On this night, I saw the Emperor Augustus at the Capitol where he had an apparition of a rainbow upon which sat the Virgin and Child. From the oracle that he caused to be interrogated upon what he had seen, he received the answer: "A Child is born, and before Him we must all flee!" The emperor at once erected an altar and offered sacrifice to the Son of the Virgin, as to the "Firstborn of God." I had also a vision of Egypt far beyond Matarea, Heliopolis, and Memphis. There was in that region a large idol that used to give answers to all kinds of questions. Suddenly it became mute. The king ordered immense sacrifices to be offered throughout his whole dominions. Then was the devil, upon the command of God, forced to say: "I have become silent, I must give place to another. The Son of the Virgin is born, and a temple will be here erected to His honor." Upon hearing this, the king wanted to raise a temple to the newborn Child next to that of the god, but I do not clearly recall the story. I know, however, that the idol was put aside and that a templewas erected to the Virgin and Child whom it had proclaimed, and who were afterward honored with pagan rites.

The visions of the three Kings leading to an actual coordination and visitation of Jesus I beheld a great wonder in the country of the Three Kings. There was a tower on a mountain to which the Kings retired in turn with a retinue of priests, in order to observe the stars. What they saw they committed to writing and communicated to one another. On this night there were two of them there, Mensor and Seir. The third, who dwelt toward the east side of the Caspian Sea (most probable Naimans, Mongolis)), was called Theokeno. He was not present. There was a certain constellation at which they always gazed, and whose variations they noted. In it they saw visions and pictures. Upon this night also, they had several visions of various kinds.

It was not in one star alone that they saw those visions, but in several that formed a figure, and there seemed to be a movement in them. They saw the vision of the moon over which arose a beautiful rainbow-colored arch on which was seated a Virgin.

The left limb was drawn up in a sitting posture, the right hung a little lower and rested on the moon. To the left of the Virgin and rising above the arch, was a grapevine, and on her right a sheaf of wheat. In front of the Virgin was a chalice like that used at the Last Supper. It appeared to issue, but with greater clearness and brightness, from the brilliancy that emanated from her.

Out of the chalice arose a Child, and over the Child shone a bright disk like an empty ostensorium. It was surrounded by radiating beams. It reminded me of the Blessed Sacrament. On the Virgin's right was an octangular church with a golden door and two small side-doors. With the right hand, the Virgin put the Child and the host into the church which, meanwhile, grew larger and larger, and in which I saw the Most Holy Trinity. Above the church arose a tower. Theokeno, the third king, had similar visions in his own home.

Over the head of the Virgin sitting on the arch shone a star, which suddenly shot from its place and skimmed along the heavens before the Kings. It was for them a voice announcing as never before that the Child, so long awaited by them and by their ancestors, was at last born in Judea, and that they were to follow that star. For some nights immediately preceding that blessed one, they had from their tower seen all kinds of visions in the heavens, kings journeying to the Child and offering their homage to Him. So now they hurriedly gathered together their treasures and with gifts and presents began the journey, for they did not want to be the last. For they do want to miss the boat that has shone to them in a very vivid supernatural way to the King of the Universe. I saw all three after a few days meeting on the way.

Who Were the Magi?

The Gospel of Matthew (2:2) tells us that "Magi from the east came to Jerusalem." Often believed to be Persian Zoroastrian astrologers and philosophers, these men were following the star of Jacob, predicted in Numbers 24:17. "*A star shall come forth out of Jacob, and a scepter shall rise out of Israel.*" Interestingly, these foreigners representing the pagan nations came to "*worship*" Jesus. Regardless of potentially taking improved trade routes south through the fertile crescent with a caravan, their journey was not likely an easy one.

The pagan foreigners came to Jerusalem, prepared to meet the King-child with precious gifts, asking "*Where is the one who has been born king of the Jews?*" Surely the Jewish people would be long awaiting the fulfillment of the prophesy, tracking the star for centuries, and know exactly when and where the newborn King was born. How odd it must have seemed to them that no one knew, and that King Herod himself summoned them in private and petitioned them to report back to him when they found the child.

Following a Star

The star led the Magi to the place of Jesus' birth, where they bowed down and worshiped him. After this, they made the dangerous decision not to return to King Herod, having been warned in a dream. Instead, they chose to go back to their country by another route.

I am not sure how many modern holy pilgrimages are set up to follow the path of the Magi, but I can't imagine that they get very many takers signing up. Certainly not the same appeal as visiting the Eternal City or the Holy Land! Although they were not Jewish, they followed the prophet Balaam's fourth message (Num 24:15-19), foretelling the coming of Christ. In fact, they were so sure of this prophesy that they traveled a great distance with gold, frankincense, and myrrh; gifts fitting a ruler. Then, upon finding the foretold "*shepherd of Israel*," these non-Jewish men bowed down and worshiped him. Finally, they hearkened to the warning in their dream not to return to Kind Herod, despite the alternate route home and the danger that could have come to them.

Source: Kimberly Cook

The Blessed Virgin foresees the approach of the Three Kings

Mary had had a vision of the approach of the three holy kings while they were resting in the tent of the King of Causur. She also saw that the latter intended to erect an altar in honor of her Child. She told this to St. Joseph and Elizabeth, and asked that they should clear out the Cave of the Nativity and make everything ready in time for the reception of the Kings. The people because of whom Mary had yesterday retreated into the other cave were visitors who had come out of curiosity. There were many such in the last few days. Today Elizabeth went home to Juttah with a servant who came to fetch her. These were quieter days in the Cave of the Nativity, and the Holy Family was generally alone. Only Mary's maidservant, a robust, serious, and unpretentious person of some thirty years, was there. She was a childless widow, related to Anna, who had given her a home. Her late husband had been very severe with her because she went so often to the Essenes, for she was very devout and was hoping for the salvation of Israel. So he was angry with her, just as today bad men are angry because their wives go to church too often. He left her and afterwards died.

In the last few days there came no more of those insistent beggars who had demanded alms at the cave with curses and abuse. They were on their way to Jerusalem for the Maccabees' Feast of the Consecration of the Temple. This feast really begins on the 25th day of the month Kislev, but as this fell on the evening of Friday, December

7th, in the year of Jesus' birth, that is to say, on the eve of the Sabbath, it was postponed to the evening of Saturday, December 8th, or the 26th day of Kislev. It lasted eight days. (Thus the sixth day after the Circumcision was the 25th day of Kislev, so that the Circumcision happened on the nineteenth day of Kislev, and Jesus' birth on the twelfth day of Kislev.) Joseph kept the Sabbath under the lamp in the Cave of the Nativity with Mary and the maidservant. On Saturday evening the Feast of the Consecration of the Temple began. Joseph had fastened lamp-brackets, in three places in the cave, on each of which he lit seven little lamps. All is quiet now; the many visitors came because they were on their way to the festival. The nurse came to Mary every day now. Anna often sends messengers with presents who take news back to her. Even when He was only a few days old the Infant Jesus was given a pap made of the pith of some rush which is light, nourishing, and sweet to taste. In the day-time the donkey is generally outside at pasture and only spends the night in the cave.

Source: Wildfire Fellowship, Inc.

Although Mary had already received so many things from her, yet the Crib Cave was still quite poor in appearance, since whatever was at all unnecessary was given away at once. Mary told Anne that the Kings from the East were approaching with rich gifts, and that their coming would attract much attention. Anne, therefore, resolved to go and stay with her sister, who dwelt at some hours' distance, and to return after the departure of the royal visitors. Then I saw Joseph set to work to clear out the Crib Cave as well as those in its vicinity, in order to prepare for the arrival of the Kings whom Mary in spirit had seen coming. He went also to Bethlehem to make the second payment of taxes and to look around for a dwelling, for he intended to settle in Bethlehem after Mary's Purification.

.Journey of the Three Kings To Bethlehem

Some days after their departure from home, I saw the caravan of Theokeno come up with those of Mensor and Seir at a ruined city (..............). Rows of tall pillars were still standing here and in many places large beautiful statues. A band of wild robbers had taken up their quarters among the ruins. They were clothed in the skins of beasts and armed with spears; they were of a brownish color, short and stout, but very agile. The three caravans left this city together at daybreak and, after journeying half a day, rested in a very fertile district where there was a spring around which were many roomy sheds. This was an ordinary halting place for caravans. Each of the Kings had in his train, as companions, four nobles of his own race; but he himself was like a patriarch over all. He took care of all, commanded all, dispensed to all. In each caravan were to be found people of different color. Mensor's race was of a pleasing brownish color; Seir's was brown; and Theokeno's of a bright yellow. I saw no shining black, saving the slaves, of whom each king possessed some.

The nobles holding staves in their hands, sat upon their dromedaries high among the piled-up packages, which were covered with hangings. These were followed by other animals almost as large as horses (..............), on which servants and slaves rode among the baggage. On their arrival, they unloaded the animals and watered them at the spring. This spring was surrounded by a little mound upon which was a wall with three open entrances.

In this enclosed space was a cistern, somewhat lower than the surrounding surface. It had a pump with three pipes furnished with faucets. Over the cistern was a cover usually kept locked. But a man from the ruined city had accompanied the travelers, and he on payment of a tax, unlocked the reservoir. The travelers had leathern vessels, which could be folded perfectly flat. They were divided into four compartments, which when filled afforded drink to four of the camels at once.

These people were extremely careful of the water; not a drop was suffered to go to waste. Then the beasts were put up in an enclosed, but uncovered space close to the spring, the stall of each animal being separated from its neighbor's by a partition. There were some troughs before them, into which was poured the feed which had been brought with them. It consisted of corn, the grains of which were as large as acorns. Among the baggage were bird baskets, high and narrow, which hung on the sides of the animals among the broad packages. In the separate compartments of these baskets, either singly or in pairs, according to their different sizes, were birds like doves or hens. They served for food on the way. In leathern chests, they had loaves, all of the same size, like single plates, closely packed together. Only as many as were needed were taken out at once. They had with them very costly vessels of yellow metal set with precious stones. They were almost exactly of the shape of our sacred vessels, some like chalices, some like little boats and dishes, out of which they drank and upon which they handed around the food. The rims of most of these vessels were set with precious stones.

The three races were somewhat different in costume. Theokeno and his followers, as well as Mensor, wore high caps embroidered in colors, and white bands wound thickly around their heads. Their short coats reached to the calf of the leg, and were very simple with only a few buttons and ornaments on the breast. They were enveloped in light, wide, and very long mantles which trailed behind. Seir and his followers wore caps with little white pads and round cowls embroidered in colors.

They had shorter mantles, which were, however, longer behind than in front. Under their mantles were short tunics buttoning down to the knee and ornamented on the breast with laces, spangles, and innumerable glittering buttons, button on button. On one side of the breast was a little sparkling shield like a star. All had bare feet bound with laces to which soles were fastened. The nobles wore short swords or large knives in their girdles, and they had many bags and boxes hanging about them. Among the Kings and their relatives were men about fifty, forty, thirty, and twenty years old. Some wore their beard long, others short. The servants and camel drivers were much more simply clothed; indeed, some had only a strip of stuff or an old garment around them. When the beasts had been fed, watered, and stalled, and the attendants themselves had drunk, a fire was made in the middle of the enclosure in which they had encamped.

The wood used for that purpose consisted of sticks about two and a half feet long which the poor people of the surrounding country had brought hither in well-arranged bundles, as if prepared expressly for travelers. The Kings constructed a three-cornered log pile and laid the sticks around the top, leaving an opening on one side to admit air. The pile was very skillfully put together. But I cannot say for certain how they lit the fire. I saw one of them put one piece of wood into another, as if into a box, swing it round and round a little while, and then draw it forth burning. And so they kindled a fire, and then I saw them killing some birds and roasting them.

The Three Kings and the ancients acted, each one in his own family, like the father of the house, cutting up the food and helping it around. The carved birds and little loaves were laid on small dishes, or plates, which stood upon little feet, and passed around; and in the same way, the cups were filled and handed to each one to drink. The lowest among the servants, of whom some were Moors, reclined on the bare earth. They appeared to be slaves. The simplicity the kindness, the good nature of the Kings and nobles, were unspeakably touching. They gave to the people who gathered around them something of all that they had; they even held out to them the golden vessels and let them drink like children.

Chapter 3

Return Home of the Three Kings

Mensor, the brownish, was a Chaldean (Persia). His city, whose name sounded to me something like Acajaja, was surrounded by a river, and appeared to be built on an island. Mensor spent most of his time in the fields with his herds. After the death of Christ, he was baptized by St. Thomas, and named Leander. Seir (Kerala, India), the brown, on that very Christmas night stood prepared at Mensor's for the expedition. He and his race were the only ones so brown, but they had red lips. The other people in the neighborhood were white. Seir had the baptism of desire. He was not living at the time of Jesus' journey to the country of the Kings. Theokeno was from Media (Naimans,Mongolia), a country more to the north. It lay like a strip of land further toward the interior and between two seas. Theokeno dwelt in his own city; its name I have forgotten. It consisted of tents erected on stone foundations. He was the wealthiest of the three. He might, I think, have taken a more direct route to Bethlehem, but in order to join the others he made a circuitous one. I think that he had even pass near Babylon in order to come up with them. He also was baptized by St. Thomas and named Leo. The names Caspar, Melchior, and Balthasar were given to the Kings, because they so well suited them, for Caspar means "He is won by love"; Melchior, "He is so coaxing, so insinuating, he uses so much address, he approaches one so gently"; Balthasar, "With his whole will, he accomplishes the will of God."

From Mensor's city, Seir dwelt at the distance of a three days' journey, each day counting twelve hours; and Theokeno further on, at a distance of five such days. Mensor and Seir were together when they saw in the stars the vision of the birth of Jesus, and both set out on the following day with their respective caravans. Theokeno, also, had the same vision in his own home, and he hurried to join the other two. Their journey to Bethlehem was about seven hundred and some odd hours. In the odd number, six occurs. It was a journey of about sixty days, each day twelve hours long (about 720 hours); but they accomplished it in thirty-three days, on account of the great speed of their camels, and because they often travelled day and night. The star that guided them was like a ball from whose lower surface light streamed as from an open mouth. It always appeared to me as if guided by an apparition that held it by a thread of light. By day I saw walking before the caravan a figure more brilliant than the light of the sun. When I reflect upon the length of the journey, the rapidity with which they made it appears to me astonishing. But those beasts have so light and even a step that their march looks to me as orderly and as swift, their movements as uniform, as the flight of birds of passage. The homes of the Three Kings formed a triangle with one another. Mensor and Seir dwelt nearest to each other; Theokeno was the most distant.

When the caravan had rested till evening, the people that had followed helped to load the beasts again, and then carried off home all that the travelers left behind them. When the caravan set out, the star was visible, shining with a reddish light, like the moon in windy weather. Its train of light was pale and long. The Kings and their followers went part of the way on foot beside their animals, praying with heads uncovered. The road here was such as to prevent their travelling quickly; but when it became level, they mounted and pushed on at a swift rate. Sometimes they slackened their pace and all sang together, the sound of their voices on the night air producing a most touching effect. When I gazed upon them riding forward in such order, their hearts filled with joy and devotion, I could not help thinking: "Ah, if our processions could only pattern after this!" Once I saw them passing the night in a field near a spring. A man from one of the huts in the neighborhood unlocked it for them. They watered their beasts and, without unpacking, refreshed themselves by a short rest.

Again I saw the caravan upon a high plateau. On their right extended a mountain chain, and it seemed to me that they were drawing near to a point in the road where it again made a descent to a thickly settled district whose houses lay among trees and fountains. The inhabitants of this place wove covers out of threads stretched from tree to tree, and adored images of oxen. They bountifully supplied food to the crowd that followed the caravan, but the dishes out of which they ate were used no more. I was surprised at that. The next day I saw the Kings near a city whose name sounded like Causur, and which was built of tents on stone foundations. They stopped to rest with the king to whom the city belonged, and whose tent palace lay at a little distance. The Three Kings had since their meeting travelled fifty-three or sixty-three hours. They told the king of Causur all that they had seen in the stars. He was very greatly astonished. He looked through a tube at the star that was guiding them, and in it he saw a little Child with a Cross.

He begged them, in consequence, to inform him on their return of all that they discovered, that he might erect altars and offer sacrifice to the Child. On the Kings' departure from Causur, they were joined by a considerable train of nobles, who were going to travel the same way. Later they rested at a spring and made a fire, but they did not unload their camels. When again on their way, I heard them softly and sweetly singing together short strophes, such as: "Over the mountains we shall go. And before the new King kneel!" One of them began and the others took up and sang with him the strophes, which they in turn compose and intoned. In the center of the star was plainly visible a little Child with a Cross. Mary had a vision of the Kings' approach when they were resting a day in Causur, and she told it to Joseph and Elizabeth.

At last I saw the Kings arrive at the first Jewish city, a small, straggling place where many of the houses were surrounded by high hedges. They were here in a straight line from Bethlehem, notwithstanding which they proceeded along toward the right as the streets ran in that direction. As they entered this place, they sang more sweetly than ever and were full of joy, for the star was here shining upon them with unusual brilliancy, although the moonlight was so bright that one could see shadows distinctly. The inhabitants of the city, however, either did not see the star, or they took no special notice of it. They were exceedingly obliging. When some of the cavalcade dismounted, they assisted them greatly in watering their camels. It reminded me of Abraham's time, for then people were all so good and ready to assist one another. Many of them, bearing branches in their hands, led the caravan through the city and even went a part of the way with them. The star was not constantly shining before them; sometimes it was quite dull. It appeared to shine out more clearly wherever good people lived; and when the travelers beheld it more brilliant than usual, their hearts were filled with emotion thinking that there, perhaps, they would find the Messiah. The Kings were not without apprehension lest their large caravan would create notice and comment.

The next day they went without halting around a dark, foggy city and, at a short distance from it, crossed a river which empties into the Dead Sea. That evening, I saw them enter a city whose name sounded like Manathea, or Madian. Their caravan was now perhaps two hundred strong, so great was the crowd their generosity drew after them. A street ran through this last place, the inhabitants of which consisted partly of Jews, partly of heathens. The caravan was led into the space between the city and its surrounding wall, and there the Kings pitched their tents. I saw here, as in the former city, how anxious they became when they discovered that no one knew anything of the newborn King, and I heard them telling how long the star had been looked for among them.

Genealogy of the Kings

I heard that the Three Kings traced their genealogy back to Job, who had dwelt on the Caucasus and had jurisdiction over other districts far and wide. Long before Balaam, and before Abraham's sojourn in Egypt, they had the prophecy of the star and the hope of its fulfillment. The leaders of a race from the land of Job had upon an expedition to Egypt, in the region of Heliopolis, received from an angel the revelation that from a virgin the Saviour would be born whom their descendants would honor. They were also instructed to go no farther, but to return to their homes and watch the stars. They celebrated festivals in memory of the event, erected altars and triumphal arches which they adorned with flowers, and then turned back home. There may, perhaps, have been three thousand of these people collected together at this time. They were dwellers in Media and star worshippers, of a beautiful, yellowish-brown color and of tall and noble stature. They roamed from place to place with their herds, ruling wherever they pleased by their irresistible power. They had, as the Kings now related, been the first to announce the prophecy to their people, and the first to introduce among them the observation of the stars. When both the prophecy and the study had fallen into general oblivion, they were received first by one of Balaam's scholars, and long after him by three prophetesses, the daughters of the Three Kings' forefathers. And now at last, five hundred years since the time of those prophetesses, the star had appeared which they were to follow.

The Three Prophetesses

Those three prophetesses were contemporary. They were deeply versed in the stars; they had visions and the spirit of prophecy. They foresaw that a star would arise out of Jacob and that an inviolate Virgin would bring forth the Saviour. Clothed in long garments, they went about the country announcing this prophecy, exhorting to good, foretelling the future down to the most remote ages, and promising that messengers from the Saviour would come to their people and lead them to the worship of the true God. The fathers of these virgins built a temple to the promised Mother of God on the spot where their lands joined, and in its vicinity a tower from which to observe the constellations and their various changes. From these three princes, about five hundred years after and through a lineal descent of fifteen generations, sprang the Holy Kings. It was by their intermingling with other races that they became so different in color. For a length of time, some of their ancestors were constantly on the tower observing the stars. What they saw was noted down and taught orally; and, in consequence of these observations, many changes gradually crept into their temple and worship.

All periods remarkable on account of their reference to the coming of the Messiah were pointed out to them by visions in the stars. During the last year since Mary's Conception, these visions were more and more significant, and the coming of salvation more explicitly shown. At the time of the Blessed Virgin's Conception, they saw the Virgin with the scepter and the scales in whose evenly balanced plates lay wheat and grapes. They saw, too, a prefiguration of the bitter Passion itself, for they beheld the newborn King involved in a war from which He came out victorious over all His enemies. This observing of the stars was accompanied by religious ceremonies, fasting, prayer, purification, and self-denial. They watched not one star alone, but a whole constellation; by certain coincidences among the different stars as they gazed, were formed the visions and pictures that they saw. The wicked, engaging in this star worship, were affected by evil influences and thrown into convulsions by their demoniacal visions. It was by the agency of such people that the practice arose of sacrificing the aged and little children. But such cruelties gradually fell into disuse. The Kings saw the visions clearly and from them tasted sweet, interior consolation, Without feeling the effects of any malign influence. They became, on the contrary, better and more pious. With great simplicity and candor, they described what they saw to their inquisitive auditors; but when they perceived that what their forefathers had so patiently awaited for two thousand years was not received with implicit belief, they became sad. The star was hidden by a cloud; but when it again appeared, looking so large among the drifting clouds and so near to the earth, the Kings arose from their couches, called the people of the city together, and pointed it out to them. The people gazed awestruck; some were deeply impressed, others were vexed at the Kings for disturbing their rest, while the majority sought but to profit by the princely bounty.

I heard the royal travelers saying how far they had journeyed up to this time. They reckoned the day's journey on foot as one of twelve hours. Before reaching their place of meeting, one had made a journey of three such days, the other five of twelve hours. But on their beasts, which were dromedaries, subtracting the night and the hours of rest, they could treble that distance; therefore the three days' journey on foot up to the place of meeting were equivalent to only one, and the five days counted but for two. From that place to where they were at present they had made a fifty-six days' journey of twelve hours, or six hundred and seventy-two hours. They had, therefore, from Christ's birth up to the present, counting the days that passed until they met and those devoted to resting, consumed about twenty-five days. At this place also, they took a day to rest.

The people here were singularly importunate and shameless; they pressed around the Kings like swarms of wasps. The royal travelers dealt out to them freely small triangular yellow pieces like tin and also darker grains. They must have possessed unnumbered treasures. When the caravan was departing, it wound around the city, in which I saw idols standing in the temple. On the opposite side they crossed a bridge and went through a little Jewish place that contained a synagogue. And now they were on a good road, hastening toward the Jordan. About one hundred persons had joined their caravan. They had still a journey of about twenty-four hours to Jerusalem. But I saw them passing through no more cities, and they were met but by few people, as it was the Sabbath. The nearer they drew to Jerusalem, the more disheartened they became; for the star no longer shone with its usual brightness and, since their entrance into Judea, they saw it but seldom. They had hoped also to find the people on their route exulting with joy and celebrating with magnificence the birth of the newborn Saviour, to honor whom they themselves had come so far. But beholding no sign of excitement, they grew anxious and perplexed, thinking that, perhaps, after all they had made a mistake. It may have been midday when they crossed the Jordan. They paid the ferrymen, though only two of them lent a helping hand. They held back[1] and let them attend to their transportation themselves. The Jordan was not broad at that time and it was full of sandbanks. Boards were laid over crossbeams, and the dromedaries stood upon them. The passage across the river was made expeditiously. The Kings first appeared to be going toward Bethlehem, but soon they turned and went on to Jerusalem. I saw the city towering up high against the sky. The Sabbath was over before the caravan arrived outside the city.

As it was the Sabbath - The Kings Before Herod

The caravan of the Kings took about a quarter of an hour to pass any given point. When it halted before Jerusalem, the star had become invisible; consequently, the travelers were very much troubled. The Kings rode upon dromedaries, and three other dromedaries were laden with the baggage. The rest of the cavalcade were mounted upon nimble animals of a yellowish color with small heads, I know not whether they were horses or asses, but they were very different in appearance from our horses. The animals upon which the nobles rode were very handsomely caparisoned and hung with golden stars and little chains. Some of the followers went to the gate of the city, and returned with officers and soldiers. The arrival of the Kings at that time when no feast was being celebrated, when no special commercial interest seemed to bring them, and also by that particular road, was something remarkable.

They explained to the officials why they had come, and spoke of the star and the Child. But their hearers were ignorant on the subject, and so the Kings began again to think that they had surely erred, since they could not find one person who looked as if he knew anything connected with the Redemption of the world. The people gazed at them in wonder, unable to conceive what they wanted. The Kings explained that they were ready to pay for whatever they got from them, and that they wished to confer with their King. And now arose great hurrying to and fro, the travelers meantime interchanging questions and answers with the crowd gathered around them. Some had indeed heard of a child that was to be born at Bethlehem; but they were poor, ignorant people, and their words had no weight. Others laughed derisively and the Kings grew troubled and disheartened; and then they perceived by the expressions of the people that Herod knew nothing of what they sought and that he was by no means beloved by his subjects. They became anxious as to how they should address him. They had recourse to prayer, their courage revived, and they said to one another: "He who has brought us so quickly here by means of the star, will also lead us home in safety." They now led the caravan around the city and brought it in at the side nearer Mount Calvary. Not far from the fish market, they and their animals were conducted into a circular court, which was surrounded by halls and dwellings, and before whose gates guards were standing. In the middle of the court was a well, at which they watered the beasts, and all found quarters in the stalls and places under the arches. On one side of the court arose the mountain on which it lay; on the other, it was free and shaded by trees. I saw people coming with torches and examining the baggage.

The Kings before Herod

Herod's palace stood higher up the mountain not far from this court. I saw the road leading to it lighted up by torches and lanterns hung on poles. I saw officials going down from the palace and conducting thither Theokeno, the eldest of the Kings. He was received under an archway and ushered into a hall. There he made known his errand to a courtier, who reported it to Herod. Herod became almost insane at the news, and gave orders for the Kings to present themselves before him on the following morning. He also sent word to them to rest while he made inquiries, and he would inform them of the result. When Theokeno returned, he and his two royal companions became still more uneasy, and ordered the baggage that had been unpacked to be packed again. They slept none that night. I saw some of them going around the city with guides. It seemed to me that they suspected Herod of knowing all, but of being unwilling to disclose the truth to them. They still sought the star. In Jerusalem itself all was quiet, but there was much running to and fro and questioning among the sentinels at the court.

It may have been about eleven o'clock at night when Theokeno was sent for by Herod. There appeared to be some kind of festivity going on, for the palace was ablaze with lights, and I saw females in it. The news brought by Theokeno threw Herod into the greatest terror. He dispatched servants to the Temple and also into the city, and I saw priests and scribes and aged Jews going to him with rolls of writings under their arms. They wore their priestly garments, also their breastplates, and their girdles on which letters were inscribed. There were about twenty around him, expounding the writings. I saw them also mounting with him to the roof of the palace and gazing at the stars. Herod was very uneasy and perplexed. But the scribes tried to divert him, by endeavoring to prove that there was nothing in the talk of the Kings; that those Eastern people were always superstitiously raving about the stars; and that, if there was any truth in what they said, surely the priests of the Temple and the dwellers in the Holy City would have known it long ago. Next morning at daybreak, I saw one of the courtiers going down to the caravan and bringing up all three of the Kings to Herod's palace. They were ushered into an apartment around which were pots of foliage and bushes. Refreshments were spread at the entrance. But the Kings declined the proffered food, and remained standing until Herod entered. They approached him with an obeisance, and without preamble put to him the question as to where they should find the newborn King of the Jews, for they had seen His star and they were come to do Him homage. Herod was very much troubled, but he concealed his fears. Some of the scribes were still with him. He questioned the Kings closely concerning the star, and told them that of Bethlehem Ephrata ran the Promise. But Mensor related to him the last vision they had seen in the star, whereupon Herod's anxiety became almost too great for concealment.

Mensor said that they had seen a Virgin with a Child lying before her. From the right side of the Child issued a branch formed of light, upon which stood a tower with many gates, **which tower increased in size until it became a city. The Child appeared standing above it with sword and scepter; and they had seen not only themselves, but all the kings of the earth, coming to bow down before and adore that Child**, for Its kingdom was to vanquish all other kingdoms. Herod advised them to go quietly and without delay to Bethlehem, and when they had found the Child to return and inform him that he too might go and adore Him. I saw the Kings going down from the palace, and leaving Jerusalem at once. The day was dawning, and the lights on the way leading up to the palace were still burning. The crowd that had followed the royal caravan had passed the night in the city.

Herod who, about the time of Christ's birth, had gone to his palace at Jericho, had been even before the coming of the Kings very restless and uneasy. Two of his illegitimate sons had been raised by him to high positions in the Temple. They were Sadducees, and by them he was kept informed of all that transpired, as well as of all who were opposed to his designs. Among these he was told of one, a man good and upright, a distinguished functionary of the Temple. Herod sent him a courteous and friendly invitation to come to him in Jericho. When the good man was on his way to comply with the invitation, Herod's creatures fell upon him and murdered him in the desert, making it appear as if robbers had perpetrated the awful deed. Some days later, Herod returned to Jerusalem, in order to take part in the Feast of the Consecration of the Temple. Then he thought he would, in his own way, give pleasure to the Jews and show them honor. He caused to be made a golden figure something like a lamb, though still more like a goat, for it had horns.

This figure was to be erected above the gate leading from the outer court of the women into the court of sacrifice. Herod insisted upon this and, moreover, expected to be thanked for what he had done. But the priests resisted. Herod threatened them with a fine. They replied that the fine indeed they would pay; but that the figure, according to their Law, they could never accept. Herod fell into a rage, and ordered it to be set up secretly. Thereupon, one of the officers of the Temple, fired with zeal, seized it as it was being brought in, cleft it in twain, and hurled it to the ground. This gave rise to a tumult, and Herod ordered the offender to be imprisoned. Herod was, on account of this affair, extremely displeased, and regretted having come to the feast; but his courtiers sought by all kinds of diversions to remove the impression from his mind.

There was among some pious people in Judea the expectation of the near advent of the Messiah, and the circumstances attendant on the birth of Jesus had been noised abroad by the shepherds. Herod had heard all and had at Bethlehem made secret inquiries into it. His spies, however, having found only poor Joseph, and having besides orders not to attract attention, reported that it was nothing, that they had found only a poor family buried in a cave, and the whole affair not worth talking about. But now, all of a sudden, appeared the great caravan of the Kings. Their questioning after the King of Judah was marked by such confidence and precision, they spoke with such certainty of the star, that Herod could scarcely hide his anxious perplexity. He hoped to learn the particulars

In her four volumes of visions of the life of Christ, Anne Catherine Emmerich says that the Magi came from the border between Chaldea and Elam, mentioning Ur, "Mozian" (Iraq's Maysan Province, anciently known as Mesene), "Sikdor" (Shushtar, near Susa), and a "city, whose name sounded to me something like Acajaja" (Aghajari), as well as other cities farther east.[60]

Country of origin and journey: according to Wikipedia

The phrase "from the east," more literally "from the rising [of the sun]", is the only information Matthew provides about the region from which they came. The Parthian Empire, centered in Iran (Persia), stretched from eastern Syria to the fringes of India. Though the empire was tolerant of other religions, its dominant religion was Zoroastrianism, with its priestly *magos* class. Although Matthew's account does not explicitly cite the motivation for their journey (other than seeing the star in the east, which they took to be the star of the King of the Jews), the apocryphal Syriac

Infancy Gospel states in its third chapter that they were pursuing a prophecy from their prophet, Zoradascht (Zoroaster).[48]

There is an Armenian tradition identifying the "Magi of Bethlehem" as Balthasar of Arabia, Melchior of Persia, and Caspar of India. Historian John of Hildesheim relates a tradition in the ancient silk road city of Taxila (in present-day Punjab, Pakistan) that one of the Magi passed through the city on the way to Bethlehem. Sebastian Brock, a historian of Christianity, has said: "It was no doubt among converts from Zoroastrianism that certain legends were developed around the Magi of the Gospels". And Anders Hultgård concluded that the Gospel story of the Magi was influenced by an Iranian legend concerning magi and a star, which was connected with Persian beliefs in the rise of a star predicting the birth of a ruler and with myths describing the manifestation of a divine figure in fire and light. There was a tradition that the Central Asian Naimans and their Christian relatives, the Keraites, were descended from the biblical Magi. This heritage passed to the Mongol dynasty of Genghis Khan when Sorghaghtani, niece of the Keraite ruler Toghrul, married Tolui, the youngest son of Genghis, and became the mother of Möngke Khan and his younger brother and successor, Kublai Khan. Toghrul became identified with the legendary Central Asian Christian king Prester John, whose Mongol descendants were sought as allies against the Muslims by contemporary European monarchs and popes.

Sempad the Constable, elder brother of King Hetoum I of Cilician Armenia, visited the Mongol court in Karakorum in 1247–1250 and in 1254. He wrote a letter to Henry I King of Cyprus and Queen Stephanie (Sempad's sister) from Samarkand in 1243, in which he said: "Tanchat [Tangut, or Western Xia], which is the land from whence came the Three Kings to Bethlehem to worship the Lord Jesus which was born. And know that the power of Christ has been, and is, so great, that the people of that land are Christians; and the whole land of Chata [Khitai, or Kara-Khitai] believes those Three Kings. I have myself been in their churches and have seen pictures of Jesus Christ and the Three Kings, one offering gold, the second frankincense, and the third myrrh. And it is through those Three Kings that they believe in Christ, and that the Chan and his people have now become Christians." The legendary Christian ruler of Central Asia Prester John was reportedly a descendant of one of the Magi.

Tombs - Journey of the Magis converted many. Source: Paul William Roberts

There are several traditions on where the remains of the Magi are located, none of which have been verified or given veracity by secular historians. Marco Polo claimed that he was shown the three tombs of the Magi at Saveh, south of Tehran in present day Iran, in the 1270s. In Persia is the city of Saba, from which the Three Magi set out when they went to worship Jesus Christ; and in this city they are buried, in three very large and beautiful monuments, side by side. And above them there is a square building, carefully kept. The bodies are still entire, with the hair and beard remaining.

The bones of the Magi are allegedly contained at the Shrine of the Three Kings at Cologne Cathedral in Germany. According to tradition, they were first discovered by Helena, mother of Constantine the Great, on her famous pilgrimage to Palestine and the Holy Lands in 326–28. She took the remains to the church of Hagia Sophia in Constantinople; in 344, they were transferred to Milan—in some accounts by the city's bishop, Eustorgius I—where they were interned in a special tomb beneath its basilica. In 1162, following the conquest of the city by Holy Roman Emperor Frederick I, the Magi's remains were transferred to Cologne Cathedral at the behest of its archbishop, Rainald von Dassel. In response to growing pilgrimages to the relics, von Dassel's successor, Philipp von Hochstaden, commissioned the current Shrine of the Three Kings in the late 12th century, which remains widely visited and venerated. The Milanese treated the fragments of masonry from their now-empty tomb as secondary relics, which were widely distributed around the region, including southern France; this accounts for the frequency with which the Magi appear on chasse reliquaries in Limoges enamel produced in the region. The city continues to celebrate its part in the tradition by holding a medieval costume parade every 6 January.

A version of this account is conveyed by 14th century cleric John of Hildesheim in *Historia Trium Regum* ("History of the Three Kings"), which begins with the journey of Helena to Jerusalem, where she recovered the True Cross and other relics: Queen Helen... began to think greatly of the bodies of these three kings, and she arrayed herself, and accompanied by many attendants, went into the Land of India after she had found the bodies of Melchior, Balthazar, and Gaspar, Queen Helen put them into one chest and ornamented it with great riches, and she brought them into Constantinople and laid them in a church that is called Saint Sophia.

Religion: Theokeno (Balthasar)

The main religion of the Naimans was shamanism and Nestorian Christianity. The Naimans that adopted Nestorianism probably converted around the same time the Keraites adopted the religion in the 11th century. They remained so after the Mongol conquest and were among the second wave of Christians to enter China with Kublai Khan. Some Nestorian Naiman fled to Kara Khitai during the Mongol conquests where some converted to Buddhism.

There was a tradition that the Naimans and their Christian relatives, the Keraites, descended from the Biblical Magi. The commander of the Mongol army that invaded Syria in 1259, Kitbuqa, was a Naiman: he is recorded to have "loved and honoured the Christians, because he was of the lineage of the Three Kings of Orient who came to

Bethlehem to adore the nativity of Our Lord." However, Kitbuqa was slain and his army decisively defeated at the Battle of Ain Jalut, ensuring continued Muslim hegemony over the Levant. Nestorianism declined and vanished among the Naiman soon after the collapse of the Yuan dynasty. Mongolian Naimans converted to Tibetan Buddhism in the sixteenth century. The Naiman assimilated into other ethnic groups living in Eurasia and likely adopted the religion and culture of the dominant group. The Naimans who settled in the western khanates of the Mongol Empire all eventually converted to Islam: Source: Wikipedia

The Free Encyclopedia Previous: Next St. Caspar (Seir) is one of the "Three Kings" along with Melchior (Mensor) and Balthasar (Theokeno), and is a character described in the Gospel of Matthew as a wise man or wise man of the Bible. The Bible does not specify who or what the Magi are, but since the 7th century, the Magi have been recognized in Western Christianity as Caspar, Melchior, and Balthazar. Caspar and two others are considered saints by the Catholic Church.

Name origin: Real Name: Seir (Casper) – Kerala, India

Caspar/Caspar/Gaspar/Jasper is generally accepted to be one of the Biblical Magi or "Three Wise Men" who are said to have visited the infant Jesus with gifts of gold, frankincense, and myrrh. However, there is some academic debate. Literature surrounding the expression of his name. These different expressions may be caused by regional and linguistic differences between scholars of different times, places, and languages. Jasper is traditionally thought to bring gold, so the Persian word jasper is a name meaning "gift-bringer" or "treasure-bearer." The name Kaspar or Kaspar is derived from the ancient ancient word "gaspar". "Gizbal" in Chaldean.

The Bible does not specify who the sorcerer was. There is only tradition. The English translation of the Bible describes them as "people who studied the stars," so it is believed that they were astrologers who were able to predict the birth of the "Messiah" from their study of the stars. Indian scholar. A 1913 Encyclopedia Britannica article states, "According to the tradition of the Western Church, Balthasar is often represented as the king of Arabia, Melchior as the king of Persia, and Caspar as the king of India." It is being Historian John Hildesheim tells of the legend of the ancient Silk Road city of Taxila, that one of the Three Wise Men passed through the city on his way to Bethlehem. Some believe that Caspar is King Gondophares (ca. 21 AD – 47 AD) from the Acts of Thomas. Others believe that he was originally from southern India, which according to tradition was visited by the Apostle Thomas decades later. A town named Piravom in the southern Indian state of Kerala has long been claimed to be where one of the three wise men of the Bible came from. The name Piravom means "birth" in the lal Malayalam language. It is believed that the name originates from a reference to the birth of Jesus.

In and around Piravom, he has concentrated three churches named after Biblical sages. In contrast, other parts of India have only three churches bearing that name. Some believe that Kaspar's kingdom was in the Egriscilla region of Upper India, a peninsula forming the east side of the Cave of Magnus (Gulf of Thailand), depicted by Johannes Schöner in his 1515 globe. Egriscilla can be seen there. In the Brahmani ("Egrisila of the Brahmins"), and in the explanatory paper that accompanied the globe, Schöner says: Indian Christian. There, the magician Gaspard was in control." The phrase "Habitat of Hiccup Rex Kaspar (Here lived King Kaspar)" is inscribed on Andreas Walsperger's Mappemonde golden Chersonese (Malay Peninsula), made in Konstanz around 1448. I am. It is also unclear whether the person who took the name Caspar was a latter-day king. is known. Some believe that the Magi were not kings now. The reference to "king" is in the Psalm, "The king of Tharsis and the islands shall bring presents; the king of Arabia and Saba shall bring him gifts: and all the kings of the earth shall bring gifts." It is thought that the word comes from the word ``deaf". I will worship him" Psalm 72:10.

Source: Father Siby Joseph of Kerala

Gift to Child Jesus

Matthew writes that the Magi brought three gifts: gold, frankincense, and myrrh. These gifts clearly have deep meanings: the gold represents Jesus' majesty, the frankincense represents his divinity, and the myrrh represents his humanity. Caspar is traditionally depicted as the middle of the three kings with a reddish beard, younger than Melchior and older than Balthazar, waiting in line behind Melchior to give the gift of frankincense to the infant Jesus. He is often depicted in the act of receiving gifts from his assistants, or removing his crown, and then representing a sign of readiness to stand at the feet of the infant Jesus.

Death: According to tradition, St. Caspar became a martyr, and some believe that the other two wise men suffered the same fate. The relics of the Magi were discovered in Persia by St. Helena, but were later taken to Constantinople and then to Milan, Italy. From there they reached Germany, where they are now housed in Cologne Cathedral. Caspar is commemorated along with other members of the Magi on Epiphany, but is also commemorated in Catholicism on his feast day, January 11th. After Caspar returned to his homeland to avoid King Herod, he is said to have celebrated Christmas in Armenia in 54 AD with other Magi magistrates. Caspar died on January 11, 55 AD, at the age of 109.

Theokeno – A Naiman, Mongolia

The Mongols, living in northeastern Mongolia, appear to have had no or little exposure to the Church of the East. Nonetheless, the Kereit, Merkit, Önggüt and Naiman became part of the Mongol state with Chinggis Khan's unification of the Mongolian plateau by 1206. Many of the spouses of the Chinggisid princes came from these tribes and continued to practice the rites of the Church of the East. There is no indication that the non-Christian spouses converted. Furthermore, the vast majority of the Mongols maintained their native beliefs. Though the Nestorians were not a majority, they played a significant role within the empire. In addition to several princesses and queens who were Christian in faith, a few high ranking officials existed in the administrative apparatus. Indeed, Ögödei Khan's (r. 1229—1240/41) primary minister, Chinqai (d. 1252) was a Nestorian Christian as were Sorqoqtani (d. 1252), a Kereit princess as well as the wife of Tolui; Töregene (d. 1246), a Naiman, and the wife Ögödei; Oghul Qaimish (d. 1252), a Merkit and wife of Güyük Khan (d. 1248) were also Nestorian Christians. Indeed, over time the papacy viewed the Christian wives of the Khans as the route to converting the Khan. The success of the missionaries in this route, however, proved minimal. Nonetheless, a Nestorian Christian influence existed in the upper circles of the empire.

As the empire expanded beyond Mongolia, the Mongols established relations with many religious communities throughout their empire for strategic as well as pragmatic reasons. Sympathetic rapport with religious elites aided in reducing the threat of hostility and rebellion among the conquered. Thus, the Mongols exempted clergy of most religions from taxes. The Mongols also often spared religious structures during invasions, unless there was resistance then no one was immune to the Mongols' wrath. Furthermore, the khans asked the clergy to pray for them. Although the clergy sometimes misinterpreted this request, within the minds of the Mongols this did not demonstrate an interest in conversion or even courting a particular religion, but rather simply respect and perhaps also interest in celestial insurance.

Source: Timothy May

Christianity among the Mongols

.The Nestorian Stele in China, erected in 781. Overall, the Mongols were highly tolerant of most religions, and typically not censored several at the same time. Though in modern times the Mongols are primarily Buddhist, during the time of the Mongol Empire they had a substantial number of Christians, many of whom were in positions of considerable power. Many Mongols had been proselytized by Christian Nestorians from the Assyrian Church of the East, since about the 7th century. When Genghis Khan, as the young Temüjin, swore allegiance with his men at the Baljuna Covenant, there were representatives of nine tribes among the 20 men. Temüjin was a shamanist, and the others included "several Christians, three Muslims, and several Buddhists." The Mongols had been proselytised by Christian Nestorians since about the 7th century and many of them were Christians. Many Mongol tribes, such as the Kerait, the Naiman, the Merkit, the Öngüd, and to a large extent the Kara Khitan, were Nestorian Christian. Under Mongka, the main religious influence was that of the Nestorians. Overall, Mongols were highly tolerant of most religions, and typically sponsored several at the same time.

Source: Religious Wiki

Origin of Mensor – Chaldean, Persia

The Gospel account contains many beautiful facts, but alas, does not provide certain crucial information. We do not know how many Magi there were. Supposition indicates that each Magus presented one of the three gifts, and therefore, there may have been three, but we do not know for certain. Nor do we know the exact location of their ancestral homeland "in the East." Because the word "magus" may be interpreted as "astronomer" or "astrologer" (from the root "M-G" meaning "star"), many suppose that they originated in either Babylon or Persia, which were famous centers of astronomy and astrology. Again, we do not know for certain. Lastly, the Gospel does not supply the names of the Magi. Later traditions assigned to them the names of Gaspar, Melchior, and Balthasar, and further traditions claimed that Gaspar was the eldest in age and Balthasar the youngest.In Western Armenian, the names are pronounced Kaspar, Melkon, and Baghdasar.

In the course of one of my arcane research ventures, I stumbled across a rare book that included a history of the Armenian Monastery of Saint John the Baptist ("Sourp Garabed Vank"), outside the ancient city of Moush. I discovered a fascinating document: It was the text of a "*Gontag*" (an official encyclical from a church functionary, from the Greek word Kontakion), asking for donations for repairs needed for a dilapidated sanctuary outside one of the villages of Moush. The *Gontag*, sadly, does not include a date or the name of the official who issued it. Nevertheless, the text, written in Classical Armenian, provides a piece of information that is both beautiful for Armenians and critical for Christianity.

As Matthew 2:12 confirms, the Magi decided to return to their homeland via a different way. According to the *Gontag*, the Magi struck northward from Bethlehem and arrived on a plain outside the ancient city of Moush. There they set up camp to rest from their weary travels. In the middle of the night, Gaspar (Seir), who was apparently the eldest of the Magi, passed away peacefully. Melchior (Mensor) and Balthasar (Theokeno) were naturally grieved by the passing of their older friend, and set upon the solemn task of arranging his proper burial. Local people were commissioned, and Gaspar (Seir) was buried at the brow of a hill overlooking the plain where they had encamped. The local people then constructed a sepulcher over the burial place. After a respectful period of mourning, Melchior and Balthasar resumed their journey home. For 300 years, the local people continued to maintain the sepulcher, and passed on the oral tradition that a wise man had seen a great star, traveled to Bethlehem, witnessed the birth of a great king, and had passed away on his return journey.

The tradition of the Magi in Armenia may also have been known to King Abgar (Apkar) of Edessa (Urfa) who, according to church history, wanted to know more about Christianity, and wrote a letter to Jesus Christ, inviting Him to come to Edessa to heal the king and remain in that city (see Eusebius, *History of the Church*). After the Resurrection, the Apostle Thaddeus journeyed to Edessa, preached about

Christianity, healed Abgar, and baptized him, making Abgar the first known Christian king of Armenia. Before Gregory the Illuminator returned to Armenia after being consecrated a bishop in Caesarea in Cappadocia, he was entrusted by Bishop Leontius with several venerated relics. As Gregory traveled back to Armenia, he stopped outside of Moush. He ordered that a monastery be constructed there to house the great relic of Saint John the Baptist. Until May, 1915, the famous Sourp Garabed Vank stood as a sentinel of Armenian Christianity.

While Gregory was sojourning in the area, the local people told him about the burial place of the wise man. At that time, the vast majority of people living around Moush were still pagan. They understood that the sepulcher contained the relics of an important person, but they were unaware of the specific connection of Gaspar (Seir) and the Magi to the theology of Christianity. Gregory immediately journeyed to the place, and recognized the sanctity of the sepulcher. He ordered that a monastery be built around the sepulcher in order to preserve and protect the relics of Gaspar (Seir). The monastery was henceforth known as "Sourp Kaspari Vank" or "Kasparavank."

Every year, on Theophany (Epiphany), when the Christmas Star appeared in the night sky, the priests, monks, and pilgrims would gather at Sourp Kaspari Vank would offer the first Holy Eucharist of the feast-day on the altar-table that was constructed over the sepulcher of Gaspar (Seir) the Wiseman. In the West, many believe the relics of the Magi were discovered in the fourth century in Milan, Italy, and were later transferred to Cologne/Koln, Germany. To this day, visitors to Cologne may see the beautiful golden shrine inside the cathedral that, according to Western tradition, preserves the remains of the Magi. For centuries, pilgrims from all over the world have flocked to Cologne at both Christmas and Epiphany to venerate these relics.

But what about Armenia? If the *Gontag* account is accurate, then it would indicate that the more important relic–the entire body of Gaspar–has been preserved and venerated in Armenia since at least the time of Gregory the Illuminator. How a fragment of this relic arrived in Europe requires serious research, and why Armenia is not accorded a superior place in the Christmas narrative remains inexplicable. Sourp Kaspari Vank appears to have functioned both as a monastery and a place of pilgrimage for Christians from the 3rd century until the early 19th century. The monastery was still visited up through 1915, although the building was apparently pillaged and ruined in the early 1800's during a series of raids by Kurdish tribes. Nevertheless, the traditional resting place of Gaspar continued to be venerated by Armenians from all around Moush and the surrounding areas. As we gather to celebrate Theophany(Epiphany) and Armenian Christmas, I hope that you will take a moment to offer a prayer for the Magi. I also hope that you will remember the many pilgrims who traveled to Sourp Kaspari Vank year after year to celebrate Armenian Christmas Eve upon the altar-table that was constructed over the sepulcher of Gaspar. I also hope that when we discuss the issue of genocide, we take into account not only the people who perished, but the precious relics that have been lost or stolen, and the centuries of cherished traditions that have vanished.

For many centuries, from at least the time of Jerome (c. 347 – 420), the term "Chaldean" was a misnomer that indicated the Biblical Aramaic language and was still the normal name in the nineteenth century Only in 1445 did it begin to be used to mean Aramaic speakers in communion with the Catholic Church, on the basis of a decree of the Council of Florence, which accepted the profession of faith that Timothy, metropolitan of the Aramaic speakers in Cyprus, made in Aramaic, and which decreed that "nobody shall in future dare to call Chaldeans, Nestorians". Previously, when there were as yet no Catholic Aramaic speakers of Mesopotamian origin, the term "Chaldean" was applied with explicit reference to their "Nestorian" religion. Thus Jacques de Vitry wrote of them in 1220/1 that "they denied that Mary was the Mother of God and claimed that Christ existed in two persons. They consecrated leavened bread and used the 'Chaldean' (Syriac) language".The decree of the Council of Florence was directed against use of "Chaldean" to signify "non-Catholic."

A Story about the Magi in Armenia – The Armenian Weekly
Source: January 6, 2012 Rev. Dr. George A. Leylegian Special Reports

The **Chaldean Catholic Church** is an Eastern Catholic particular church (*sui iuris*) in full communion with the Holy See and the rest of the Catholic Church, and is headed by the Chaldean Patriarchate. Employing in its liturgy the East Syriac Rite in the Syriac dialect of the Aramaic language, it is part of Syriac Christianity. Headquartered in the Cathedral of Our Lady of Sorrows, Baghdad, Iraq, since 1950, it is headed by the Catholicos-Patriarch Louis Raphaël I Sako. In 2010, it had a membership of 490,371, of whom 310,235 (63.27%) lived in the Middle East (mainly in Iraq).

The United States Commission on International Religious Freedom reports that, according to the Iraqi Christian Foundation, an agency of the Chaldean Catholic Church, approximately 80% of Iraqi Christians are of that church. In its own 2018 Report on Religious Freedom, the United States Department of State put the Chaldean Catholics at approximately 67% of the Christians in Iraq. The 2019

Country Guidance on Iraq of the European Union Agency for Asylum gives the same information as the United States Department of State.

The Church's relations with its fellow Assyrians in the Assyrian Church of the East have improved in recent years. In 1994, Pope John Paul II and Patriarch Dinkha IV of the Assyrian Church of the East signed a *Common Christological Declaration*. On the 20 July 2001, the Holy See issued a document, in agreement with the Assyrian Church of the East, named *Guidelines for admission to the Eucharist between the Chaldean Church and the Assyrian Church of the East*, which confirmed also the validity of the Anaphora of Addai and Mari. Mensor (Melchoir) did his job and helped many converted to the Catholic Faith.

Appendix

Fullness of Truth in the Catholic Church

History shows that Jesus founded the Catholic Church to teach in His name. Although elements of truth exist elsewhere, the fullness of truth subsists only within the Catholic Church. It does not mean that only the Catholics can be saved. Other religions possess various degrees of the truth.

Thanks to God and my parents I was born a Catholic. I am 80 years old and I feel my Faith is still growing. This is why I am writing this story.

Here is concrete and physical reason why I am Catholic.

♥ Let us start with the Bible. No Book in the history of the world has wielded as much influence on civilization as the Holy Bible. The Bible is unique in that it had God as its Author, while all other books were composed by human beings. The Council of Hippo in AD 393 determine which books were inspired and were to be included in the Bible Canon. God made first the alliance with the Patriarchs and then with the Jewish people through Moses, a Saviour is promised and a Law is proclaimed, and salvation is through the Law. The New Testament is the covenant or the alliance that God made with all men whereby, through the mediatorship of His Son, Jesus Christ, all men can be saved.

♥ The existence of Jesus Christ is foretold and prophesied by many: Matthew 2:1-12; Isaiah 60:3; Psalm 72:10; Numbers 24:17; Numbers 24:15-19; Daniel 9:25; Micah 5:2; Isaiah 7:14;Matthew 1:18-23; Isaiah 9:6; Micah 5:2.

♥Emperor Shun (2230 B.C.) believed in one God called Shangdi who was the supreme ruler of the universe. Shangdi means "Emperor", "Supreme Deity" or "Highest Deity". Shangdi was never made into an idol or image. The Emperor functioned not only as ruler but also as high priest. Emperor Guang Wu reigned during the time of Christ's death and resurrection. The fact that he and astronomers knew Christ was God is shown in Chinese historical records dated around A.D 31. "Eclipse on the day of Gui Hai, Man from Heaven died". History of Latter Han, Annals, No. 18, Gui Hai. As we know, when Christ died there was darkness that covered the earth. "From the sixth hour until the ninth hour darkness came over all the land." Mark 15:33.

Source: Wikipedia

♥Many scholars have said that based on academic standards, Jesus and His resurrection are one of the strongest and most proven events of history. But did you know that Chinese scholars from the time of Jesus also were given evidence that Jesus was born, died and rose again as a perfect sacrifice to bring pardon for man's sin and a whole new era of human history? Pastor Kong Hee from Singapore found some of this evidence and spoke about it. The evidence dates back to the very time that Jesus was living, but it is evidence from China. I found links to the original Chinese documents with help from a couple Chinese friends and a couple more intriguing facts from China that also are evidence of Jesus life on earth while I was in China. We already have evidence and proof for Jesus' resurrection way beyond reasonable about according to many scholars. Even non-Christian scholars like Bart Ehrman agree that the evidence for the resurrection is better than the evidence for miracles in any other religion.

♥But this evidence from China is unique because it comes from cosmological sources which are beyond any human control and also ancient Chinese classics which have been verified by the atheist Chinese government as reliable history. It is also from a country far distant from Israel and from the same time Jesus lived. That should be logical enough to help eliminate any remaining doubt as to the fact that Jesus was born, died and rose again and that He cares enough to give evidence of His divinity to people in many cultures/nations throughout the world (researchers have documented evidence for God independent of the Bible in at least 300 major cultures).

Source: Bryan Bissell

♥The three Holy Kings were known as in astronomy, mathematics, and governance and they all played a crucial role in the development of early human culture and technology. Somehow, they manage to come together with Seir from India and Theokeno from Mongolia. Their common traits are they are wise rulers possessing the knowledge to predict and prophesy what is going on in the World. Possessing these God given gifts, they got to learn of the birth of Christ and made preparations to meet each other for the long journey to Bethlehem. Their gifts to the birth of Jesus: The three gifts had a spiritual meaning: gold as a symbol of kinship on earth, frankincense (an incense) as a symbol of deity, and myrrh (an embalming oil) as a symbol of death. This dates back to Origen in Contra Celsum: "gold, as to a king; myrrh, as to one who was mortal; and incense, as to a God."

Source: Wikipedia

Shroud of Turin: From Wikipedia, the free encyclopedia

♥The **Shroud of Turin** (Italian: *Sindone di Torino*), also known as the **Holy Shroud** (Italian: *Sacra Sindone*), is a length of linen cloth that bears a faint image of the front and back of a man. It has been venerated for centuries, especially by members of the Catholic Church, as the actual burial shroud used to wrap the body of Jesus of Nazareth after his crucifixion, and upon which Jesus's bodily image is miraculously imprinted. The human image on the shroud can be discerned more clearly in a black and white photographic negative than in its natural sepia color, an effect discovered in 1898 by Secondo Pia, who produced the first photographs of the shroud. This negative image is associated with a popular Catholic devotion to the Holy Face of Jesus. The shroud's authenticity as a holy relic has been disputed even within the Catholic Church, and radiocarbon dating has shown it to be a medieval artifact, the image on which could be produced by differential exposure of a chemically prepared fabric to bright sunlight (and all of the fabric is expected to slowly become darker in the future).

From Wikipedia, the free encyclopedia the Sudarium of Oviedo.

♥The **Sudarium of Oviedo**, or **Shroud of Oviedo**,

is a bloodstained piece of cloth measuring c. 84 x 53 cm (33 x 21 inches) kept in the Cámara Santa of the Cathedral of San Salvador , Oviedo, Spain. The Sudarium (Latin for sweat cloth) is thought to be the cloth that was wrapped around the head of Jesus Christ after he died as described in John 20:6–7. The cloth has been dated to around 700 AD by radiocarbon dating. However, at the same conference at which this information was presented, it was noted that in actuality the cloth has a definite history extending back to approximately 570 AD. The laboratory noted that later oil contamination could have resulted in the late dating. The small chapel housing it was built specifically for the cloth by King Alfonso II of Asturias in AD 840; the Arca Santa is an elaborate reliquary chest with a Romanesque metal frontal for the storage of the Sudarium and other relics. The Sudarium is displayed to the public three times a year: Good Friday, the Feast of the Triumph of the Cross on 14 September, and its octave on 21 September.

THE RELICS OF THE PASSION

♥**The Cross:** The veneration of the True Cross finds its origin with St. Helen, mother of Emperor Constantine, who said to have unearthed three crosses at Golgotha about 300 years after then Crucifixion. She verified though a series of miracles which was the True Cross of Christ. Pilgrims returning from Jerusalem, and later from Rome, took relics with them and disseminated them in different parts of the world. Some of these relics are kept in the Basilica of Santa Croce in Jerusalem, in Rome.

♥**Crown of Thorns.** The Crown was documented as being in Jerusalem in 409 AD. It was transferred to Constantinople in 1063, although the thorns were removed presented to various rulers in Europe at an earlier date. In 1238 Baldwin II, the Latin Emperor of Constantinoble, anxious to obtain support for his empire offered the crown of thorns to Louis IX, King of France, who built the Sainte-Chapelle to house it. During the French Revolution, the crown was kept in the Bibliotheque Nationale until 1806 when the thornless remains were deposited in the Cathedral of Notre Dame in Paris. Two thorns are in the Church of Santa Croce.

♥**The Nails:** The nails were also discovered by St. Helen, one nail was tossed into the Adriatic to calm a storm. The other two were used by the Empress to protect her son. One was placed in his crown and another formed into a bridle for his horse. Filings were taken from the true nails and imbedded in copies to make relics of a lower class. Some of these are presented as true nails rather than copies but the one kept at the Basilica of Santa Croce is authentic.

♥**The Titulus:** A part of the title of the Cross bearing the words 'Jesus of Nazareth, King of the Jews" is found in Santa Croce. There are sources indicating that such a relic was venerated in the courtyard on Calvary in Jerusalem. The pilgrim Aetheria (9c. 385) mentions this. St. Helen is said to have divided the relic into three parts, giving one to Constantine, keeping one in Jerusalem and sending the last to Rome.

♥**The Lance:** St. Longinus' lance has been divided. The shaft of the lance is at St. Peter's Basilica, Rome. The head of the spear is claimed by two different places. One is claimed by the Hofburg Treasure House, Vienna, Austria. Another story says that the Emperor Baldwin II sent the point to Venice as a pledge for a loan of money. St. Louis, King of France, redeemed this relic, and brought it to Paris, where it is kept in St. Chapelle.

♥**Veronica's Veil:** Veronica kept the veil and discovered its curative properties. It is said that she cured Emperor Tiberius with it, then left it in the care of Pope Clement (the fourth Pope) and his successors. It has been in the hands of the Church ever since and is kept now in the Basilica of St. Peter.

♥Lourdes: n 1858, the Virgin Mary allegedly appeared to Bernadette Soubirous (Maria Bernada Sobirós in her native Occitan language) on a total of eighteen occasions at Lourdes (Lorda in her local Occitan language). Lourdes has become a major place of Roman Catholic pilgrimage and of miraculous healings. The 150th Jubilee of the first apparition took place on 11 February 2008 with an outdoor Mass attended by approximately 45,000 pilgrims. In 2020, Lourdes had a population of around 15,000. In 2012, 715,000 pilgrims attended Our Lady of Lourdes related events, falling to 570,000 in 2016.[12] In 2011, Lourdes contained about 270 hotels, the second-greatest number of hotels per square kilometer in France after Paris.[13] Its deluxe hotels include Grand Hotel Moderne, Hotel Grand de la Grotte, Hotel St. Étienne, Hotel Majestic, and Hotel Roissy

In the evening of February 11, 1858, a young Roman Catholic girl, Bernadette Soubirous, reported that she went to fetch some firewood with her sister and another companion when a Lady who was indescribably beautiful appeared to her at the Massabielle grotto. Although the Lady did not tell Bernadette her name when asked at first, she told her to return to the grotto. On subsequent visits, the Lady revealed herself to be the "Immaculate Conception". This was a reference to the dogma of the Immaculate Conception which had been defined only four years earlier in 1854 by Pope Pius IX, stating that the Virgin Mary herself had been conceived free from the consequences of original sin. Bernadette, having only a rudimentary knowledge of the Catholic faith, did not understand what this meant, but she reported it to her parish priest, Father Peyremale. Peyremale, though initially very skeptical of Bernadette's claims, became convinced by hearing this because he knew that the young girl had no knowledge of the doctrine.

The Lady also told Bernadette to dig in the ground at a certain spot and to drink from the small spring of water that began to bubble up. Almost immediately cures were reported from the water. Today thousands of gallons of water gush from the source of the spring, and pilgrims are able to bathe in it. Countless purported miracle cures have been documented there, from the healing of nervous disorders and cancers to cases of paralysis and even of blindness. During the apparitions, Bernadette Soubirous prayed the Rosary. Pope John Paul II wrote: "The Rosary of the Virgin Mary [is] a prayer of great significance, destined to bring forth a harvest of holiness": .Source: Wikipedia

♥Fatima: During World War I, Pope Benedict XV made repeated but forlorn pleas for peace, and finally in May 1917, made a direct appeal to the Blessed Mother to intercede for peace in the world. Just over a week later, Our Lady began to appear at Fatima, Portugal to three shepherd children: Lucia dos Santos, age 10, and her cousins, Francisco and Jacinta Marto, ages 9 and 7. Fatima is a small village about 70 miles north of Lisbon.

The Promised Miracle:

The greatest miracle to occur since the Resurrection is also the only miracle ever precisely predicted as to date, time of day and location. While popularly known as "The Miracle of the Sun," October 13, 1917 has come to be known as "The Day the Sun Danced," the headline of the article by Almeida in *O Seculo*. During the solar phenomena, the sun whirled and zig-zagged, casting colors about the crowd as it began to descend toward the earth. The 70,000 people assembled cried out in terror, thinking it was the end of the world. After about 10 minutes, the sun returned to the sky. Then a howling wind began to blow, despite the leaves on the trees remaining still. The rain-soaked people were suddenly dry and their clothes clean, and the ground was completely dry. Many physical cures of the blind and the lame were reported. The countless unreserved public confessions of sin and commitments to conversion of life attest to the authenticity of what they saw. The miracle is reported to have been seen from as far as 15-25 miles away, thus ruling out the possibility of any type of collective hallucination or mass hypnotism. No such phenomenon of the sun was reported anywhere in the world, and scientists were unable to explain it. Doubters and skeptics had become believers. Even the on-site reporter, Almeida, stood by his story later on in spite of harsh criticism. (See translation of Almeida's article)

Source: World of Apostolate of Fatima, USA

Our Lady's image on the Tilma

♥Our Lady of Guadalupe appeared in Mexico as the pregnant Mother of God to Blessed Juan Diego, and Aztec Indian, on December 9, 10, and 12, 1531. She left a Miraculous Image of her appearance of his cactus fiber cloak, or tilma, which still exists today for all to see in the Basilica of Our Lady of Guadalupe in Mexico City. Our Lady came to offer faith, hope an consolation to the oppressed natives of Mexico and to reconcile then with their Spanish rulers. She put an end to the bloody human sacrifice of the Aztecs and converted ten million natives in the next 10 years! There were many more apparitions of our Holy Mother Mary, as our Lady of La Salette, our Lady of Garabandal, Medjugorje and even appeared to me Her lowly servant

July 22, 2012 at Saint Peter Chanel Catholic Church. Our Lord Jesus Christ also appeared to many: as Sacred Heart of Jesus in Paris, Faustina in Poland and many more even to me whilst I am sitting in a dentist chair for 3 hours on October 15, 2014 and our Lord Jesus appeared to me in a vision 3 times to console and comfort me. It was to St. Margaret Mary Alacoque, a humble nun of the Order of the Visitation of Our Lady that Our Lord chose to reveal to the world His Sacred Heart, thus opening a New Era of Grace and Mercy in the history of the Church and the world.

The Incorruptibles

♥"Incorruptible" is a term used to describe a body that has fully or partially resisted the natural decomposition process after death. The phenomenon is not common, but there are more than 300 saints whose bodies were exhumed decades or even centuries after their death, and showed no signs of physical decay. In Mauritius, where my father was born, Pere La Valle's body has been incorrupt for 200 years. Our Saints keep appearing to many and we have 37 royalties who have been canonized as saints. I have written and compiled two books about royalties who have been canonized saints. (Please read Holy Kings, Holy Queens, Holy Royalties Volume I and II).

Source: National Shrine of Mother Mary

♥**The Holy Eucharist**: The Holy Eucharist is a central sacrament in our Catholic faith, as we believe it is the body and blood of Jesus Christ. According to Church teaching, during the celebration of the Eucharist, the bread and wine offered by the faithful are transformed into the body and blood of Christ through a process called transubstantiation. In his writings on the Eucharist, Fr. Spitzer reminds us that a Eucharistic miracle occurs every day, at every Holy Mass across the world when the substance of bread and wine is transformed into the substance of Jesus' body and blood. However, the term **"Eucharistic miracle" can also refer to extraordinary empirical signs of Jesus' presence in the Eucharist, such as bleeding hosts or the transubstation of a consecrated host into a piece of cardiac muscle tissue.**

"For us believers what we have seen is something that we have always believed. . . If our Lord is speaking to us by giving us this sign, it certainly needs a response from us." —Bishop Cyril Mar Baselice, Archbishop of the diocese of Trivandrum on the Eucharistic Miracle at Chirattakonam, India

Some notable Eucharistic miracles happened years and years ago (i.e., the Eucharistic Miracle of Lanciano, Italy, in the 8th century and the Eucharistic

Miracle of Santarem, Portugal, in the 13th century). Others have happened in more recent history, such as the scientifically proven Eucharistic miracles of Buenos Aires in 1992-1996. However, there is a handful that have taken place in just the past twenty years. Below are four stories of approved and recent Eucharistic miracles:

The Eucharistic Miracle at Legnica: A Bleeding Host

♥On Christmas Day 2013, at the Church of Saint Hyacinth in Legnica, Poland, a consecrated host fell on the floor. The host was put into a container with water so that it would dissolve. Instead, it formed red stains. In Feb. 2014, the host was examined by various research institutes, including the Department of Forensic Medicine in Szczecin, stated:

"In the histopathological image, the fragments were found containing the fragmented parts of the cross-striated muscle. It is most similar to the heart muscle."

Additionally, and similar to the findings of the Eucharistic miracle of Lanciano, Italy, the research found that the tissue had alterations that would appear during great distress. The bleeding Host in Poland was approved for veneration in April 2016 by Bishop Zbigniew Kiernikowski of Legnica, who said that it "has the hallmarks of a Eucharistic miracle." Learn more here.

The Eucharistic Miracle in Tixtla, Mexico

♥In Oct. 2006, a parish in the Chilpancingo-Chilapa Diocese of Mexico held a retreat. During mass, two priests and a religious sister were distributing communion when the religious sister looked at the celebrant with tears in her eyes. The Host that she held had begun to effuse a reddish substance. To determine the validity of the event, Bishop Alejo Zavala Castro asked Dr. Ricardo Castañón Gómez (who researched the Eucharistic miracle in Buenos Aires) and his team to conduct scientific research.

In 2013, the research concluded that:

"The reddish substance analyzed corresponds to blood in which there are hemoglobin and DNA of human origin. . . The blood type is AB, similar to the one found in the Host of Lanciano and in the Holy Shroud of Turin."

A Eucharistic Miracle at Chirattakonam, India, 2001

♥Though most Eucharistic miracles have to do with a bleeding host, the one at Chirattakonam, India, was a bit different. On an April morning in 2001, Fr. Johnson Karoor, pastor at St. Mary's parish in Chirattakonam, India, exposed the Blessed Sacrament for adoration. Soon, Fr. Karoor noticed three dots on the host and shared what he saw with the people, who also saw the dots. The priest then left for a week and came back to find that the host had developed an image of a human face. To ensure it wasn't his imagination, he asked an alternate server if he saw anything in the host. "I see the figure of a man," the altar server replied. After Mass, Fr. Karoor had a local photographer capture the image of the host below:

The Eucharistic Miracle in Sokolka, Poland

♥Before the bleeding host in Legnica, there was another Eucharistic miracle in Poland that occurred in the city of Sokolka. The miracle took place in 2008 at the church of St. Anthony. That morning during Mass, a priest accidentally dropped a host while distributing Communion. The Host was then put in a small container of water. The pastor, Fr. Stanislaw Gniedziejko, asked the sacristan, Sister Julia Dubowska of the Congregation of the Eucharistic Sisters, to place the container in a safe in the sacristy. After a week, Sister Julia checked on the host. When she opened the safe, she smelled something like unleavened bread, and the host had a red blood stain on it.

Immediately, Sister Julia and Fr. Gniedziejko told the archbishop of Bialystok, Bishop Edward Ozorowski, about the host. The Bishop had the stained host taken out of the container and placed on a corporal, where it stayed in the tabernacle for three years. During this time, the stained fragment of the host dried out (appearing more like a blood stain or clot), and several studies were commissioned on the host. The studies found that the altered fragment of the host is identical to the myocardial (heart) tissue of a person who is nearing death. Additionally, the structure of the muscle fibers and that of the bread are interwoven in a way impossible to produce by human means. Also, continue to learn in the second volume of the *Called Out of Darkness Trilogy*, read Fr. Spitzer's book, *Escape from Evil's Darkness*. This book presents evidence that Jesus established just one Church, with Peter as its head. Fr. Spitzer shows that the Catholic Church—with its rich array of sacraments, teachings, prayer traditions, and lived examples of holiness—continues to be fertile ground for profound Christian conversion.

Source: Magis Center

A new eucharistic miracle in Latin America?:

♥By ACI Prensa: A corporal (sacred linen cloth) at a small rural chapel in Honduras showed large stains that seemed to be of..**Connecticut church:** By Zelda Caldwell:"They were running out of hosts and all of a sudden more hosts were there.

A new eucharistic miracle in Mexico? By David Ramos: A video circulating on social media shows what appears to be a eucharistic miracle — a consecrated Host exposed for.

♥I personally met 2 priests, **Father John Struzzo** and **Father Jeremy Paulin** who experienced Eucharist Miracles. Father Struzzo was a Chaplain in our Pilgrimage to Holy Land and he experienced the Eucharist turned to blood. Father Paulin was just ordained and on his first Mass, he experienced the Eucharist turn to blood. There are many Eucharistic Miracles, some are reported and some are not.

Source: National Shrine of Mother Mary

By Father Rich Tomkosky

Our Lady appeared to **Sister Agnes Sasagawa**, part of the religious community, the Eucharistic Handmaids of the Sacred Heart, in 1973 in the snowy mountain city of Akita in northern Japan. Sister Agnes was 42 years old when this occurred, and she is still living at the age of 92 in seclusion in Japan. She was a convert from Buddhism and was half deaf at the time. Sister Agnes first encountered the Heavenly realm at a time of Adoration of the Blessed Sacrament. A very bright light engulfed her when the Tabernacle was opened. She was so overwhelmed, she prostrated herself on the floor of the chapel. This continued over the course of three days leading up to the Solemnity of Corpus Christi.

She asked the other Sisters if they saw the luminous light from the Tabernacle and they said, "No." Sister Agnes also saw angels worship the Holy Eucharist in a circle around the Altar. Sister Agnes reported the experience to Bishop Ito, the local Bishop, who was visiting the sisters at that time. He advised her to keep the experience quiet and see what happens next. Our Lady then appeared three specific times in 1973 to Sister Agnes on July 6, August 3, and October 13. I will briefly touch upon them, but to read more in detail checkout: https://www.ewtn.com/catholicism/library/message-from-our-lady–akita-japan-5167. On July 6, Our Lady told Sister Agnes that her deafness was an opportunity to offer reparation for all the sins of the world; she was completely healed of her deafness in 1982 by God. Our Lady then prayed with Sister Agnes the beautiful prayer Bishop Ito had written that the sisters prayed in thanksgiving for the Eucharist every day.

Luz de María de Bonilla is a Catholic mystic, stigmatist, wife, mother, Third Order Augustinian, and prophet from Costa Rica, currently residing in Argentina. She grew up in a very religious home with great devotion to the Eucharist, and as a child, experienced heavenly visits from her guardian angel and the Blessed mother, whom she considered her companions and confidants. In 1990, she received a miraculous healing from an illness, coinciding with both a visitation from the Blessed Mother and a new and more public calling to share her mystical experiences. Soon she would fall into profound ecstasy not only in the presence of her family—her husband and eight children, but also of people close to her who began to gather to pray; and they, in turn, formed a prayer cenacle, which accompanies her to this day.

After years of abandoning herself to the will of God, Luz de María began to suffer the pain of the Cross, which she carries in her body and soul. This first happened, she shared, on Good Friday: "Our Lord asked me if I wanted to participate in His sufferings. I answered affirmatively, and then after a day of continuous prayer, that night, Christ appeared to me on the Cross and shared His wounds. It was indescribable pain, although I know that however painful it may be, it is not the totality of the pain that Christ continues to suffer for humanity." It was on March 19 of 1992, that the Blessed Mother began to speak regularly to Luz de María. Since then, she has mostly received two messages per week and on occasion, only one. The messages originally came as internal locutions, followed by visions of Mary, who came to describe Luz de María's mission. "I had never seen so much beauty," Luz said of Mary's appearance. "It's something you can never get used to. Each time is like the first."

Several months later, Mary and Saint Michael the Archangel introduced her to Our Lord in a vision, and in time, Jesus and Mary would speak to her of coming events, such as the Warning. The messages went from being private to public, and by divine command, she must communicate them to the world.

Exorcist, Healer and Mystic Father Jim Blount

Exorcist and healing ministry priest Fr. James Blount, SOLT, of the Archdiocese of Atlanta, Ga., explained visions he allegedly experienced of the Blessed Virgin Mary in the sky. Fr. Blount said he experienced **three visions in the same day of Our Lady** "high up in the sky." The priest added that he and his religious community are all consecrated to the Blessed Virgin Mary. "I've been in love with her for a long time," Fr. Blount explains. "She is the woman of my life. She is unutterably beautiful. Mother Angelica once said that when the angels look at Our Lady, they swoon–they gasp for breath at her beauty." "I long for the day when everyone knows this reality of God's "Mona Lisa," His finest creation."

Mother Mary Angelica Foundress - EWTN

They say God works in mysterious ways, but no one would have predicted He would choose a Poor Clare nun with no broadcasting experience to build a media empire.

EWTN's future foundress was born on April 20, 1923. Young Rita Rizzo experienced two miracles that would shape her later life. Through them, she realized God loved her personally, and she began to love him back. In 1944, she entered a convent and became Sister Mary Angelica. After a series of crippling ailments, she promised God if He would allow her to walk again, she would start a monastery in the South.

In those early days, survival was a challenge for Our Lady of the Angels monastery in Irondale, Alabama. To support their work, the sisters sold fishing lures and roasted peanuts, and Mother Angelica gave parlor talks, using her wit and charm to win over the audience. As she gained popularity, Mother was frequently invited to speak to groups or on radio. But it was on a visit to a Baptist run television station in Chicago where she famously declared "Lord, I gotta have one of these."

Armed with only $200, and 12 cloistered nuns with no television background, Mother turned the monastery's garage into a television studio. In 1981, EWTN went on the air as the country's first Catholic satellite television station. Mother became a television star hosting a popular and still running show, "Mother Angelica Live." Despite innumerable challenges and millions in debt, the network grew supported only by viewer contributions.

Today, EWTN is the largest Catholic media corporation in the world. Its 11 TV channnels are broadcast in multiple languages to over 425 million TV households in more than 160 countries and territories. With extensive efforts in newsgathering, radio, newspapers, websites and publishing, it spreads the Gospel of Jesus Christ to a worldwide audience desperately searching for the Truth.

All because of one nun who refused to take "no" for an answer, and instead relied on God to provide.

There are many visionaries, mystics, and prophets currently all approved by our Catholic Church. We have also Medjugorje where ongoing 6 visionaries talk to our Holy Mother Mary, it is not approved yet.

Revelations Paperback – May 31, 2022

by Xavier Reyes-Ayral (Author)
4.8 *4.8 out of 5 stars* 803 ratings

4.5 on Goodreads
Amazon

From 1846 to the present day, the Vatican has maintained quite the same message brought forth from Heaven by different messengers across time and across vast distances and continents. This message echoes the gravest of admonitions and calls mankind to convert and find refuge through the knowledge of the truth, which today threatens the very basis of world peace...

Today, in 2022, the message of La Salette, La Fraudais, Tilly, Fatima, Garabandal, Akita and Medjugorje, and their secrets take a meaning of the greatest importance, as the admonitions brought forth by the Blessed Virgin Mary warn of a cataclysmic global disaster which has now become imminent. The Church's apprehension of frightening the masses, inspired inaction and Rome's decision to silence – founded more on fear than on caution – led millions of faithful to the darkness of ignorance and, therefore, to a lack of necessary conversion, prayers and intercession for peace. This book proposes unveiling the light and, thus, asking humanity to respond to the call of a warm and loving mother who merely seeks the salvation of her children.

During Jesus' three year ministry together with the apostles, He said to Peter " Peter, I am here to speak the truth, to stand against evil, and to allow God's love to all. I am here to show the Way and to show it may upset some, but it will save many!

The most powerful reason I am a Catholic is because the more devoted, faithful and loving to Jesus Christ, in turn he inspires me, guides me, directs me and protects me. Our Lord Jesus Christ is always with His Church until the end of time.

Revelations from heaven: Wake up!

The divine reconquest over Church's infiltration begins now

A religious order that has been receiving messages from heaven for 30 years has finally direction and hope to the faithful in this perilous and confusing time.

John-Henry
Westen
Wed Feb 28, 2024 - 11:21 am EST
Listen to this article
0:00 / 11:36
1X
Beyond Words

(LifeSiteNews) — The world and the Church today are in a state of confusion such that at no other time in human history does Our Lord's warning in Matthew 24:24 ring true: "Even the elect, if possible, will be deceived." At this time, where especially the leaders in the one true Church of Christ are silent and many betray, there is no longer an earthly solution to the crisis. But God has always revealed His works to the prophets, even to our day. As we read in the Holy Bible: "For the Lord God doth nothing without revealing his secret to his servants the prophets" (Amos 3:7).

I was blessed by a providential encounter with Fr. John Mary Foster of the Mission of Divine Mercy in Texas who had discerned he was to reach out to me regarding the messages from heaven his religious community has received about our times. Most importantly the messages from Our Lord and Our Lady reveal that the heavenly reconquest of the Church which has been infiltrated begins NOW. And they also say that the Church today is without a shepherd.

Below you will find the full message released today. And for the next two Wednesdays, March 6 and March 13, tune in to LifeSiteNews.com at 11:00am Eastern for the release of the next two messages which the Mission of Divine Mercy feels Our Lord calling them to reveal to mankind.

Our Blessed Mother, Jesus. A call to all the children of God.
February 8, 2024

Note: This writing was given to me at the Teocalli, on Tepeyac (at the Mission). I was told to go there and that there They would dictate it to me.

[Our Blessed Mother] I will speak first, daughter. Write. From My new Tepeyac I speak to you, children. From My Sanctuary I send you My Love and My Consolation, and once more I tell you to look at My Son and to do everything that He tells you to do. He is the living Word of the Father, His Love made flesh for you. Children, the battle looms and you are asleep. I come to awake you; as a good Mother who, being vigilant and keeping watch over Her children, and seeing the increasing danger, shakes her children so that they may not perish without fighting.

Children, these are the times announced from of old, in which the thrice cursed serpent will poison many, and meddle in what is Ours, and will rise to confuse the nations with his puppets, his servants, to destroy all that is of God and to take His place and sovereignty. His longing to be adored and his hatred for God have motivated him to prepare for centuries what is now being unveiled before your eyes. I have come to you, children, time and time again, year after year, to warn you, to call you to the battle, to give you weapons with which to fight and defeat Satan's works.

But how few of you have listened to Me. How few of you have understood Me and placed yourselves at My disposal in order for Me to form My luminous army. How few, children. How few. From My new Tepeyac – yes, new, for from here will flow the great River of Grace to reconquer all of the children of God – from this little piece of land, hidden, rough, I call out to you once more. Children, there is no time left. The battle, Our counterattack begins. It begins with these Words, which We give to you as Light, Protection, Guidance and consolation. Our Words. Do not ignore them. Receive them and welcome them into your souls. They will give you Light to see in the darkness of the confusion that now reigns in the Church and in the world.

US Canada Catholic

They will give you the Guidance that you need, now that My Church is without a shepherd to tend to My sheep, to My children. They will give you the protection that you need against all the attacks of those who have clothed themselves in sheep's clothing and in false meekness, but who are ravenous wolves that are devouring My children without pity – confusing, distorting the supreme and radiant Truth to then destroy the souls of My children. On guard, My children. You are hated because you are children of God and Mine. They want to destroy you, children.

Arise with Me to fight and defend, to uncover and with Me to crush the filthy devil in his pride. And receive My Words of Love and consolation You are wounded, My little children; some more, some less, but all of you carry wounds – [from] your own decisions; [from] the hatred of Satan – and all of you need Our Healing, all of you need Our help.

My children, I give My Jesus to you again. I give Him to you with all My personal Love. I give Him to you as your King. I give Him to you as your Savior and Redeemer. I give Him to you as your Captain. As your Master. As your Refuge and Protection.

Jesus. Jesus. Jesus.

Only Him, children. Only He saves. Only He Purifies. Only He heals. There is no other, children. Do not be confused. Many voices try and will try to pass as His. Many say and will say that they do everything in His Name. But look at their works. Look at the fruits, children. DO NOT IGNORE THEM.

The Father Most Holy has given all authority and all judgement to the Son. Only His Name saves, children. There is no other name. Before Him shall all knees bend and all foreheads bow.

HE IS. THERE IS NO OTHER.

Children, open your eyes and look at your God. Keep your gaze steadfast on Him. Lay aside your thoughts and human criteria, for they are infected by the reigning lack of Faith. And I, your Mother, will take you by the hand and will prepare your soul to receive the supreme Gift that is the beautiful and radiant simple Faith that gives life to everything in your being. You need this luminous Faith in the center of your soul to be able to face the present and coming times, in which everything that seemed to be stable will crumble down. You need this Faith to be able to receive all that We desire to give you, and that you need in order to work in Our Plan and be instruments of Grace for all your brothers who still live in the darkness of the separation from God.

Come to Me, My little children, I am your Mother, full of Love for Her little ones. I clasp you to My Heart and I bring you in My arms to My Jesus. Do not refuse this Gift of Mine, children. Do not refuse this time of Grace. After the last call comes the cry of the trumpet that begins the great battle. All that takes place is a preparation for this battle, and you need to be prepared. You have been created for these times and for this battle. And I, your Mother and your Queen, remind you of it.

Amen. The times have come.

And Our God arises with Power.

Blessed is he who receives these Words and allows them to bear their fruit. Blessed is he who abandons himself to Me and allows Me to form him. He will be a worthy soldier of the Divine Word Who descends once again to make His Truth shine.

The Eternal Truth, luminous, Imperishable.

Children, with Me and with all the heavenly hosts, let us adore
Him Who Is, Who Was, and Who Is to Come.
The Father, the All-Mighty.
The Son, the Redeemer.
The Most Holy Spirit of God, the Sanctifier and Restorer.
To the One and Triune God be all praise, honor, glory and power,
For ever and ever.

Amen.

Listen to My Voice, little children.
Your Heavenly Mother,
Mary Most Holy, your Immaculate Queen,
Who, together with you, will crush the head of the filthy serpent. Amen.

Now Jesus continues

Now I, your Lord and God, speak to you. I speak to you from this Throne of Mine, this little hill in which I will show My Power and My Love. Look at My Cross, children. What do you see? My absolute Obedience. My total abandonment. The living Testimony given to the Words and to the Will of My Father. The Seal with My Blood over the Eternal Truth, unchangeable and ever fruitful.

The fulfilment of the entrusted Mission for the good of humanity and all that has come forth from the Heart of the Father. The Perfect cooperation with the Plan of the Father – the Plan of Mercy, Plan of Grace, Plan of Restitution and Vindication. Look again. What do you see? My pierced hands, feet, and side. The pain that is offered – the complete Offering of body, soul, and spirit – that is consumed to the last step, the last drop, the last effort, to be faithful to the Will of the Father.

The COMPLETE Offering. The Offering to which you unite your sorrows, sufferings and efforts. The great Offering that bears continuous fruit, and that now reaches its fullness. Everything, children, is prepared in Faith, in Obedience, in Humility, and in Pain. I have given you an example with My life.

WITH MY LIFE AND WITH MY DEATH AND WITH MY RESURRECTION.

Follow Me.

Follow Me in this tremendous Hour, when – as in that Friday in which all of the powers of the devil united to torment Me and put Me to death – they now come together once more to torment and put My Church, My Mystical Body, to death; and thus give death to all that belongs to God. Satan has never ceased longing to be adored. And what you see now is his plan to supplant God in everything. I let him show his plan, uncover his servants and his machinations, so that you can see them. So that you can realize who he is and where he has infiltrated himself.

Children, he has infiltrated EVERYTHING. And he thinks that he will have dominion over all. And I must let him continue to believe thus, while I gather My army to destroy his works at the appointed Hour. This is the Hour, children. I call you to My army. I speak to you and I will speak to you, do not reject My Voice. My Voice will thunder and will resound, and will destroy every work of Satan.

Open your eyes and your ears to these words of Mine. Your God speaks to you. He speaks to you from His Throne in Heaven, He speaks to call you and awake you. He speaks to console your pain of feeling abandoned.

YOUR GOD SPEAKS TO YOU.

Listen to Me, children. Listen to Me.

Your Jesus

The Divine Word Who speaks to you here and now.

I could not find a better word to translate "inmiscuir," which in Spanish has a more negative connotation, especially in the sense in who Our Lady is using it – like saying that the enemy sneaks himself into everything, in a very conniving way. At least that is my sense of how the word is being used

FOLLOW JOHN-HENRY

John-Henry is the co-founder, CEO and editor-in-chief of LifeSiteNews.com. He and his wife Dianne have eight children and they live in the Ottawa Valley in Ontario, Canada. He has spoken at conferences and retreats, and appeared on radio and television throughout the world. John-Henry founded the Rome Life Forum, an annual strategy meeting for life, faith and family leaders worldwide. He is a board member of the John Paul II Academy for Human Life and the Family. He is a consultant to Canada's largest pro-life organization Campaign Life Coalition, and serves on the executive of the Ontario branch of the organization. He has run three times for political office in the province of Ontario representing the Family Coalition Party. John-Henry earned an MA from the University of Toronto in School and Child Clinical Psychology and an Honours BA from York University in Psychology.

Gospel: John 3 14-21

Jesus said to Nicodemus: "Just as Moses lifted up the serpent in the desert, so must the Son of Man be lifted up, so that everyone who believes in him may have eternal life." For God so loved the world that he gave his only Son, so that everyone who believes in him might not perish but might have eternal life. For God did not send his Son into the world to condemn the world, but that the world might be saved through Him. Whoever believes in Him will not be condemned, but whoever does not believe has already been condemned, because he has not believed in the name of the only Son of God.

And this is the verdict, that the light came into the world, but people preferred darkness to light, because their works were evil. For everyone who does wicked things hates the light and does not come toward the light, so that his works might not be exposed. But whoever lives the truth comes to the light, so that his works may be clearly seen as done in God. We need to do our part and help build the kingdom of God. In humility let us ask and place before the Holy Spirit our gifts, charisms, and ministries. Let us strive to keep the unity and share God's love and life with all. Pray for wisdom to understand our mission. Pray for God's grace to carry out His work.

Who is a witness to Jesus as the Son of God – Source Father Siby Joseph

Does Jesus need to provide witness to him being the Son of God? This is the question that Jesus is trying to answer in today's passage. Who is a witness to Jesus? John the Baptist is the main person who bears witness to Jesus. He was respected as a prophet and since he was from the Levitical priestly lineage, he was well-received by many even though his methods were non-traditional. Jesus affirms that John's witness is true but he goes on further to say that God the Father directly bears witness to Jesus being his Son. But how does the Father bear witness to the Son? - By doing great works through Jesus. His works are a witness that the Father is blessing the hands of his Son. But even though the people see his work, they do not recognize God in it and thus do not recognize His Son.

We fail to recognize God and therefore fail to act in His ways even today. Even though we read about and see the great works of God and know his commandments, for us to live a good and faithful life; we tend to corrupt ourselves. Therefore, in Exodus, God sends Moses to teach the people to get back on track. The people of Israel went astray because they kept forgetting that God had done great things for them. They keep turning to idols. They do not recognize God and do not believe.

Knowingly or unknowingly we are all in search of eternal life or to find meaning in life because that is how God created us. But we keep searching for life in worldly things. We must remember that we will not find life in any of these but in the Lord alone - in a relationship with him, in a friendship with him. Therefore let us not be fooled by the distractions, idols and doubts that the world throws at us. Let us do what Jesus did in rebuking Satan when he tempted him. He used the word of God - truth to fight temptation. When we do this, we will recognize Jesus as our Lord and we will be his witnesses to a world that still needs witnesses for Jesus.

The end.

www.ingramcontent.com/pod-product-compliance
Ingram Content Group UK Ltd.
Pitfield, Milton Keynes, MK11 3LW, UK
UKHW062008290726
14090UKWH00022B/1457